Knowing God
Making God the Main Thing in My Life

Knowing God

Making God the Main Thing in My Life

Participant's Workbook

Kimberly Dunnam Reisman

Abingdon Press / Nashville

SISTERS:
KNOWING GOD, MAKING GOD THE MAIN THING IN MY LIFE

Copyright © 2003 by Abingdon Press

This book is printed on acid-free, elemental chlorine-free paper.

Library of Congress Cataloging-in-Publication Data

Reisman, Kimberly Dunnam, 1960–
    Knowing God : making God the main thing in my life : participant's
workbook / Kimberly Dunnam Reisman.
        p. cm. – (Sisters)
Includes bibliographical references (p.   ).
    ISBN 0-687-02727-6 (pbk.)
1. Christian women—Prayer-books and devotions—English.   I. Title.
II. Series.

    BV4844.R45 2003
    248.8'43—dc21   2003005565

Scripture quotations taken from the *Holy Bible,* New Living Translation, copyright © 1996. Used by permission of Tyndale House Publishers, Inc., Wheaton, Illinois 60189. All rights reserved.

Scripture taken from *THE MESSAGE.* Copyright © Eugene H. Peterson, 1993, 1994, 1995. Used by permission of NavPress Publishing Group.

Scriptures quoted from *The Holy Bible, New Century Version,* copyright © 1987, 1988, 1991 by Word Publishing, Nashville, Tennessee 37214. Used by permission.

Scripture quotations from New Revised Standard Version of the Bible, copyright 1989, Division of Christian Education of the National Council of Churches of Christ in the United States of America. Used by permission. All rights reserved.

Scripture taken from the Holy Bible, Today's New International Version ^{TM}. Copyright © 2001 by International Bible Society. All rights reserved.

Scripture taken from the HOLY BIBLE, NEW INTERNATIONAL VERSION ®. Copyright © 1973, 1978, 1984 by International Bible Society. Used by permission of Zondervan Publishing House. All rights reserved.

Excerpts from THE JERUSALEM BIBLE, copyright © 1966 by Darton, Longman & Todd, Ltd. and Doubleday, a division of Random House, Inc. Reprinted by Permission.

Excerpts from THE NEW JERUSALEM BIBLE, copyright © 1985 by Darton, Longman & Todd, Ltd. and Doubleday, a division of Random House, Inc. Reprinted by Permission.

Scripture taken from the New King James Version. Copyright © 1982 by Thomas Nelson, Inc. Used by permission. All rights reserved.

ISBN 13: 978-0-687-02707-1

07 08 09 10 11 12—10 9 8
MANUFACTURED IN THE UNITED STATES OF AMERICA

To my children,

Nathan, Maggie, and Hannah,

who have blessed me with an abundance of joy and love

Contents

INTRODUCTION   11

WEEK ONE: THE CLUES WE NEED
Day One: God's Self-communication   17
Day Two: The Breath of God   21
Day Three: The Space Between the Notes   26
Day Four: The Word of God   30
Day Five: Absolute Truth   33
Day Six: The Path of God   36
Day Seven: The Breath, the Word, the Path   39
Group Meeting for Week One   41

WEEK TWO: WHAT FAITH WE HAVE
Day One: Who Is This God?   45
Day Two: Our Point of Departure   48
Day Three: The First Step on the Journey   51
Day Four: Our Gigantic Secret   54
Day Five: Who Am I?   58
Day Six: I Am Kim   62
Day Seven: What Faith We Have   65
Group Meeting for Week Two   68

WEEK THREE: SHAPING THE INVISIBLE

Day One: The Right Connections 71

Day Two: Outstretched Hands, Inches Apart 74

Day Three: Harnessed 77

Day Four: The Answering Place 81

Day Five: Trusting Our Instincts 84

Day Six: Praying from the Heart 87

Day Seven: Creating the Yet to Be 90

Group Meeting for Week Three 93

WEEK FOUR: A LIFE OF MORAL EXCELLENCE

Day One: Useful Knowledge 97

Day Two: Empowering Grace 101

Day Three: Bearing Fruit 104

Day Four: Hearing and Doing 107

Day Five: Christ at the Center 112

Day Six: The Peace of Christ 117

Day Seven: The Divine Disconnect 121

Group Meeting for Week Four 124

WEEK FIVE: DIVINE DESTINY

Day One: Our Kingdom Niche 127

Day Two: Locked On 130

Day Three: What's Holding You Back? 133

Day Four: Our Own Worst Enemy 136

Day Five: The Power to Do 140

Day Six: Bigger than You 144

Day Seven: When Did All These Baseball Players Get Here? 148

Group Meeting for Week Five 151

WEEK SIX: THE BIG PICTURE

Day One: Stories Rather than Models   153
Day Two: Competing Stories, Part One   157
Day Three: Competing Stories, Part Two   162
Day Four: What Sort of Tale Have We Fallen Into?   167
Day Five: Actors, Not Writers   171
Day Six: For Such a Time as This   174
Day Seven: The Climax   178
Group Meeting for Week Six   182

HELPFUL REMINDERS   185

BIBLIOGRAPHY   189

Introduction

As I have moved through ministry, much of my energy has been invested in reaching out to unchurched and pre-Christian people. One of the weaknesses of the church over the last half of the 20th century has been its general inability to communicate the gospel in ways that are relevant to the existing culture. We seem to have taken for granted that people will hear and understand the gospel message, and that they will be able to connect it meaningfully to their lives. This assumption has led to the loss of millions of people as we have failed to make clear connections between faith and the rest of life. My ministry has focused on making those connections—on presenting the gospel message in ways that are relevant to life in this postmodern age.

We live in an era in which faith is not automatic. While in the past we in the church might have presumed that faith would be passed on in a natural way from parents to their children, this is no longer the case. As Colleen Carroll, author of *The New Faithful: Why Young Adults Are Embracing Christian Orthodoxy*, has said in an interview with *Christianity Today* (August 5, 2002; page 42), faith is "not something embedded in [the] family anymore." Faith has become for many a conscious choice. Our culture questions us everyday; thus, gone are the days when it was possible to embrace faith without questioning it at all. The good news is that people, young and old, are embracing faith. The difficulty lies in living out that faith in the midst of a culture that at its best simply gives lip service to and at its worst is antagonistic toward that same faith.

This culture within which we must live out our faith is filled with voices seeking to separate faith from the rest of American life. It appears that society would rather interpret the US constitution as supporting freedom *from* religion, divorcing faith from all but the most private of situations, rather than recognizing that it calls for freedom *of* religion, which is a vastly different idea indeed. I serve on the Human Relations Commission of my small town. This role connected me with a larger countywide effort to create a "diversity roundtable" dedicated to education and networking, the goal being to create a community environment where "everyone has the opportunity to be safe, healthy, productive and happy . . . [by promoting] strategies that encourage acceptance of diversity . . . across the lifespan." (*Vision 2020: A Plan for the Future of Greater Lafayette,* August 2001; pages 15–16) During a meeting where we discussed the concept of a roundtable, a woman mentioned her fear of religious folks bringing "hidden agendas" to this forum. I questioned that comment, stating that while I had no "hidden agenda" in participating, my perspective was decidedly Christian, my faith informed my outlook on all of life, and that if I was required to deny that or check it at the door, I would be no more able to do so than I would be to ignore the fact that I was a woman. Not surprisingly, the reaction to my comment was mixed, with visible signs of relief that attitudes of faith would be respected, but with signs as well that diversity, at least in the minds of some, does not include the recognition of any type of faith perspective.

The reality is that it is impossible to dissociate faith from our daily lives. Whether we are conscious of it or not, our faith—what we believe about God —has an impact on how we live our lives. Our faith (or lack of it) influences our choices; and in complementary fashion, our choices influence our ability (or inability) to grow and develop our faith. This workbook is an attempt to deepen our relationship with God and with others, to grow our faith in ways that strengthen our ability to live God's teachings and make us more aware of the connections between faith and daily life. The title, *Knowing God: Making God the Main Thing in My Life,* is suggestive of that goal. Many things clamor for our attention. Many demands are placed upon our lives. Many choices lay before us as life unfolds. If we are to live lives grounded in faith, we must develop strategies for centering ourselves on God and ordering our lives around God's guiding presence.

Such an endeavor requires spiritual exploration at many levels. It is not merely enough to look at God's teachings as they are found in Scripture. Making God the main thing is more than simply applying a list of teachings the way we might apply advice from a self-help book. Examining our attitudes toward Scripture itself is a first step in that process. Understanding the role and authority Scripture has for us as God's chosen means of self-communication is crucial if we are to bridge the gap between Scripture and our daily lives.

Making God the main thing also requires that we explore our existing relationship with God. Who is this God that we believe in? How has our relationship with this God unfolded in our lives? Who are we in relationship to this God? These are but a few of the avenues of discovery necessary if we are to move God into the center of our lives.

Finally, we must look clearly at our lives as we are currently living them, the choices we are making, the commitments we have undertaken, and our views about how our lives fit into the larger world picture. Examining where God fits in at this point in our lives will be helpful in discovering what steps we need to take to strengthen our relationship with God and to place that relationship at the center of our commitments. Exploring why God inhabits a particular part of our lives and not another, or the whole, will give us insight as we continue our spiritual journey. Discovering God's purpose for our lives and the gifts we have to offer others will enable us to live out God's teachings more effectively and enhance our ability to connect our faith with daily living.

I believe God has created each of us with a unique purpose and destiny. God desires us to experience the meaning and fulfillment that come when we live our lives in sync with that purpose and destiny. Coming to know God and making God the main thing in our lives is crucial if we are to move toward the future God intends for us. It is at the heart of finding meaning and fulfillment. Yet it is not for our benefit alone. God desires us to live lives of significance and depth in order that we might be a channel of God's power in our world. Thus, as we connect our personal life of faith with the outer activities of our daily life, God's kingdom will become more fully realized not only within us but also through us.

THE PLAN

This workbook is designed for individual and group use; therefore a word is necessary about the process. It is simple but very important.

It has been my experience in teaching and ministering with small groups that a six-to-eight-week period for a group study is manageable and effective. Also, persons can generally best appropriate content and truth in small doses. This is the reason for organizing the material in segments to be read daily.

The plan for this workbook is common to other studies that I have written that call for a six-week commitment. You are asked to give about thirty minutes each day to read and reflect on the topics covered in that day's segment. For most persons, the thirty minutes will come at the beginning of the day. However, if it is not possible for you to give the time at the beginning of the day, do it whenever the time is available. The most important part of daily study is not when it happens, but *that* it happens, and regularly. This is not only an intellectual pursuit; it is a spiritual journey in order that you might incorporate the content into your daily life as you seek to make God the main thing.

It is a personal journey, but one that you will share with other women who share the desire to deepen their relationship with God and who will meet together once each week during the six weeks of the study.

The workbook is divided into six major sections, each designed to guide you for one week. These sections contain seven segments corresponding to each day of the week. Each day of the week includes three major facets: *reading, reflecting,* and *recording ideas and thoughts* about the material and your own understanding and experience, and some practical suggestions for incorporating ideas from the reading material into your daily life.

In each daily segment, you will read something about knowing God and making God the main thing in your life. It will not be too much to read, but it will be enough to challenge thought and action.

When including quotations from sources other than Scripture, I have tried to provide the author's name and page number on which the quote can be found. These citations correspond to the bibliography at the back of the workbook, allowing you the opportunity to read certain works more fully should you be interested in doing so.

Throughout the workbook you will see this symbol ✱ When you come to the symbol, please stop. Don't read any further; think and reflect according to the instructions in order to internalize the ideas being shared or the experience reflected upon.

Reflecting and Recording

After the reading each day, there will be a time for reflecting and recording. This dimension calls for you to record some of your reflections. Space is provided for you to write your thoughts in response to the questions. All the questions are designed with the assumption that you will write a response. The value of writing comes at several levels. Writing encourages us to be deliberate about our thoughts in order to put them on paper; in addition, writing our thoughts and feelings enables us to go back at a later time, which frequently adds to our spiritual growth.

The degree of meaning you receive from this workbook is largely dependent upon your faithfulness to its practice. There may be days in which you are unable to do precisely what is requested. If that is the case, simply make note of that fact and why you cannot follow through. Doing so may give you some insight about yourself and help you to grow. Also on some days, there may be more suggestions than you can deal with in the time you have. Do what is most meaningful for you and do not feel guilty.

Finally, always remember that you are on a personal journey. What you write in your workbook is your private property. You may not wish to share it with anyone. For this reason, no two people should attempt to share the same workbook. The importance of what you write is not what it may mean to someone else, but what it means to you. Writing, even if it is only brief notes or single-word reminders, helps us clarify our feelings and thinking.

The significance of the reflecting and recording dimension will grow as you move through the study. Even beyond the six weeks, you will find meaning in looking back to what you wrote on a particular day in response to a particular situation.

Sharing with Others

In the history of Christian spirituality, the spiritual director or guide has been a significant person. To varying degrees, most of us have had spiritual directors —persons to whom we have turned for support and direction on our spiritual journey. There is a sense in which this workbook can be a spiritual guide; however, the meaning will be enhanced if you share the adventure with eight to twelve other women. In this way, you will profit from the growing insights of others, and they will profit from yours. Moreover, several suggestions are included at the end of each week to help you prepare for the group interaction.

Since this is a group endeavor, everyone should begin her personal involvement with the workbook on the same day, so that when you come together to share as a group, all of you will have been dealing with the same material and will be at the same place in the text. Group sessions are designed to last approximately one and one-half hours. Those sharing in the group should covenant to attend all sessions unless an emergency prevents attendance. There will be six weekly sessions in addition to an initial get-acquainted time.

Week One:
The Clues We Need

DAY ONE: GOD'S SELF-COMMUNICATION

All Scripture is inspired by God and is useful to teach us what is true and to make us realize what is wrong in our lives. It straightens us out and teaches us to do what is right. It is God's way of preparing us in every way, fully equipped for every good thing God wants us to do.
(2 Timothy 3:16-17, New Living Translation*)*

If one of the goals of our journey together is to grow our faith in ways that strengthen our ability to live God's teachings and thus enhance the connection between faith and daily life, the best place to begin is with Scripture itself—the place where we find God's teaching. Looking at Scripture is important not simply to locate God's teaching in an effort to apply it to our lives. Exploring the Bible is important because discovering how we feel about Scripture, its role in influencing our choices, and the power and authority we give it over our decision-making processes will have an impact on our ability to make God the main thing.

I often teach DISCIPLE: BECOMING DISCIPLES THROUGH BIBLE STUDY, a rigorous 34-week study of the Old and New Testaments. In the first session, we raise the question of attention to Scripture. When do we usually attend to it? When do we most often ignore it? More often than not, folks respond that we usually attend to Scripture when we are in need or struggling. Invariably, people agree that we most often ignore Scripture when its message to us is inconvenient or goes against our preconceived notions or inclinations.

As Christians, we believe the Bible is God's chosen means of self-communication. It is one of the ways in which God continues to reveal God's self to us in the midst of our current situation. Our sincerity in viewing Scripture this way will determine our success in making God the main thing. Some of us do not always associate the God with whom we feel intimate with the God we read about in the Bible. There can be for some a gap between the God we experience in worship or in our devotional life and the God who inhabits our sacred stories of faith, which are so frequently dominated by male characters, male authors, and the patriarchal perspective of the ancient world. Yet, dedicating ourselves to a genuine understanding of Scripture as a means of God's self-communication, as a means through which God is active *now*, not just in the realm of ancient times, opens us to the reality that God's voice transcends not only all primeval perspectives but our own post-modern perspective as well. Rather than viewing the God of Scripture as captured somehow in the pages of an antiquated book, we will be aware of the variety of ways in which God desires to speak to us—through Scripture, worship, and prayer.

Understanding Scripture as God's means of self-communication is hindered by the view of some that the biblical word is constraining rather than life giving. It is as though we believe God is trying to hog-tie us with this complex and sometimes confusing jumble of teachings. If we are disposed to view Scripture in this way, our path toward making God the main thing will be much more difficult, filled with roadblocks of rationalization and self-justification when God's Word does not easily fit into our existing worldview.

Thomas Hobbes's metaphor of the hedge fence is helpful in freeing us from a "hog-tying" sense of Scripture. Many centuries ago, the hedge fence grew on each side of the king's highway. It was placed there not to stop travelers but to keep them safely on the path. Anyone could jump the hedge to take a shortcut, but they did so at their own risk. Leaving the highway meant traveling through open country where there were no maps and many unforeseen dangers.

The Bible provides a hedge as we travel on the spiritual highway. There are many places where the hedge is distinct—the Ten Commandments for example. Jumping the hedge is always a possibility; but then we will be on our own in open country. There will be few maps and many risks. Unfortunately, there are also places where we cannot always discern the hedge, places where it is sparse and indistinct. It is not always easy to apply biblical teaching to our current world situation. That moral ambiguity, however, should not be an excuse to jump over clearly marked and well-defined hedges. As Christians we affirm that moral principles do exist, principles that are always right and that breaking them is always wrong.

Rather than constraining us, Scripture provides a hedge to protect us as we journey, providing us with a safe arena in which to face the moral ambiguities that are an unavoidable part of living. Respect for God is the beginning of wisdom. When we move to an understanding of Scripture as God's means of communicating with us *for our benefit,* we will be more committed to connecting all of Scripture to our daily lives rather than just the parts that are convenient, or that fit into our current mode of thinking.

Reflecting and Recording

Spend some time thinking about how you feel about Scripture, its role in influencing your choices, the power and authority you give it over your decision-making processes.

$$*$$

When do you usually attend to Scripture? Describe a situation in your life when you attended to Scripture. Why did you behave in this way? How did you feel about this experience?

When do you usually ignore Scripture? Describe a situation in your life when you ignored Scripture. Why did you make these choices? How did you feel about this experience?

Reflect on the idea that the Bible is God's means of self-communication, that God is active in speaking to us through Scripture *now*, and that God's self-communication is *for our benefit.*

✳

Spend a few minutes in prayer. Pray that the life-giving power of God's Word will be revealed to you as you begin this study.

During the Day

Be aware of situations in which you are inclined to ignore God's Word. Make note of your thoughts and reasons for choosing to ignore.

DAY TWO: THE BREATH OF GOD

God, teach me lessons for living
so I can stay the course.
Give me insight so I can do what you tell me—
my whole life one long, obedient response.
Guide me down the road of your commandments;
I love traveling this freeway!
Give me a bent for your words of wisdom,
and not for piling up loot.
Divert my eyes from toys and trinkets,
invigorate me on the pilgrim way.
Affirm your promises to me—
promises made to all who fear you.
(Psalm 119:33-38, THE MESSAGE)

Indiana Jones is one of my favorite adventure film characters. In the third installment of the Indiana Jones movie series, *Indiana Jones and the Last Crusade,* Harrison Ford returns as Indiana Jones, the World War II-era daredevil archeologist who time and again battles Nazi evildoers. In the *Last Crusade,* Indy's father, played by Sean Connery, joins him in his adventures. Indy's father has devoted his life to searching for the Holy Grail. According to legend, anyone who drinks from the Holy Grail, the cup used by Christ at the Last Supper, will never die. During his lifelong search, Indy's father has kept a diary. All the clues that he has discovered, instructions, maps, drawings, everything needed to solve the mystery of the whereabouts of the Grail, is included in this special book. Not surprisingly, the Nazis are searching for the Grail as well and have heard of this special diary. As the exciting events of the movie unfold, the book changes hands several times, and we follow the adventures of Indy and his father as they race the Nazis for the Holy Grail.

At one point, Indy and his father, following the clues in the diary, are headed for Alexandria. Indy's father reads from the diary, "When we get to Alexandria, we will face these challenges. First, the breath of God, only the penitent man may pass. Second, the word of God, only in the footsteps of God will he succeed. Third, the path of God, only in the leap from the lion's head will he prove his worth." (*Indiana Jones and the Last Crusade,* Paramount Pictures/ Lucasfilm, Ltd., 1989)

This scene is meaningful for me because it illustrates what the Bible is all about—*the breath of God, the word of God, the path of God.* The Bible is more than a book, more even than a collection of books. The Bible is the breath of God. This is not a new idea, and reading it often brings to mind the view of Scripture as divinely inspired. This is true. Many years ago, God inspired folks to write what we now hold as our sacred Scripture. But that is not the whole story. That is not what moves me when I think of Scripture as the breath of God —as God-breathed.

When I speak of the Bible as being the breath of God, I'm talking about something alive and dynamic. The breath of God is what animates all of creation. The breath of God is what brought Adam and Eve to life and thus into relationship with God. The breath of God is interactive, energetic, vibrant. Thus, for me, asserting my belief that all Scripture is God-breathed is asserting that not just many years ago, but *right now,* Scripture is alive with God's breath and able to speak to us.

Look at today's reading from Psalm 119. The psalmist desires to be immersed in God's word, to understand God's teaching, to make "my whole life one long, obedient response" (verse 34, *THE MESSAGE*). This is not a desire for some future time, nor is it a reflection on an earlier time of insight. It is a present-tense desire, a desire that *right now,* in this moment, God's word would permeate the psalmist's entire being. Understanding Scripture as God-breathed is to understand that it is a present-tense experience. When we unite our voice with that of the psalmist, we are not simply reciting an ancient prayer; we are praying in the present tense, with an implied *now.* Teach me, give me insight, guide me . . . *now.*

The God-breathed nature of Scripture, its present-tense quality, becomes real for me over and over again as I read and reread the Bible. I am aware of the fact that Scripture is alive with the breath of God each time I read a familiar passage and come away with a slightly different understanding, one that fits my need at that particular moment.

I recall attending a clergy meeting with Bishop Woodie White of the North Indiana Conference of The United Methodist Church. To begin our time together, he gave a devotional on a story in Luke 5. A crowd had gathered around Jesus while he was standing beside the lake of Gennesaret. There were fishermen who were nearby washing their nets after a night of fishing. Jesus saw their empty boats and decided to use them for his purposes.

> *He got into one of the boats, the one belonging to Simon, and asked him to put out a little way from the shore. Then he sat down and taught the crowds from the boat. When he had finished speaking, he said to Simon, "Put out into the deep water and let down your nets for a catch." Simon answered, "Master, we have worked all night long but have caught nothing. Yet if you say so, I will let down the nets." When they had done this, they caught so many fish that their nets were beginning to break. So they signaled their partners in the other boat to come and help them.*
>
> *(Luke 5:3-7, New Revised Standard Version)*

As Bishop White began to speak on this passage, I wondered what his focus would be. We were meeting in the weeks following September 11, 2001, and I remember feeling a great deal of pressure to meet the needs of my congregation in those turbulent days. I recall feeling slightly distracted as I wondered how he would be able to speak to my need through this passage. It was not that I did not appreciate the story. Aspects of it had been very meaningful for me over the years. Jesus' request that Peter move into "deeper water" has always been a challenging word for me. Peter's obedience in letting down the nets even though he was tired and didn't think it would be a fruitful endeavor has always been a source of encouragement. Yet neither of those elements of the story jumped out at me. Nothing seemed to speak to me as the bishop continued his talk.

Then I had the distinct awareness that the story had changed. It was nothing specific. Bishop White had actually reached the end. He had mentioned the deeper water; he had highlighted Peter's obedience in the midst of fatigue. He was simply wrapping it up by rereading what happened when Peter obeyed: "They caught so many fish their nets were beginning to break." But then he stopped and asked us to pay special attention, and as I listened I could feel the Scripture coming alive for me. I could feel God's breath as it moved toward me from the text. "So they signaled their partners . . . to come and help them."

My need in that moment was in front of me. I had felt alone in my attempts to lead my congregation through tumultuous times. I had believed that I alone carried the weight of giving them guidance in the midst of tragedy and spiritual questioning. But I was not alone. I had partners that I could signal for help. The breath of God awakened in me the need to reach out for support during those difficult days.

The Bible is like Indy's father's diary—it has all the clues we need to negotiate our journey of faith. It is God's diary and holds the very breath of God. Making God the main thing begins with an openness to experiencing God breathing through Scripture, an openness to experiencing the dynamic, vibrant, "right now" quality of God's Word. As we seek to move God to the center of our lives, we need to be aware of the movement of God's Spirit breathing through the Word and be open to its power to touch us in the uniqueness of every situation in our lives.

Reflecting and Recording

Describe a time when Scripture touched you at an important point of need.

List several Scripture passages that have been meaningful to you. Make note of the variety of ways each passage has touched you.

During the Day

Paul reminded Timothy that "all Scripture is God-breathed and is useful for teaching, rebuking, correcting, and training in righteousness, so that all God's people may be thoroughly equipped for every good work." (2 Timothy 3:16-17, Today's New International Version) This is a helpful reminder of the aliveness of Scripture. You can find this passage reprinted in the back of this workbook. Cut it out and put it somewhere where you will see it on a regular basis as a reminder of God's desire to speak to you through Scripture *right now.*

DAY THREE: THE SPACE BETWEEN THE NOTES

Jesus returned to the Mount of Olives, but early the next morning he was back again at the Temple. A crowd soon gathered, and he sat down and taught them. As he was speaking, the teachers of religious law and Pharisees brought a woman they had caught in the act of adultery. They put her in front of the crowd.

"Teacher," they said to Jesus, "this woman was caught in the very act of adultery. The law of Moses says to stone her. What do you say?"

They were trying to trap him into saying something they could use against him, but Jesus stooped down and wrote in the dust with his finger. They kept demanding an answer, so he stood up again and said, "All right, stone her. But let those who have never sinned throw the first stones!"
(John 8:1-7, New Living Translation*)*

One of my mentors is Michael Slaughter, pastor of Ginghamsburg Church in Tipp City, Ohio. His work is on the cutting edge of ministry to unchurched folks, and I look to him often for inspiration and guidance. In a sermon several years ago he drew a parallel between the Bible and jazz. I immediately fell in love with that metaphor, because I too love music. Slaughter said that the coolest thing about jazz is that it is not as much about the notes as it is about what happens *between* the notes. That is where the parallel between the Bible and jazz is so vivid. The Bible is like jazz, because it is not just about the verses; it is about being in tune to what God is saying *between* the verses.

The story about Jesus and the woman caught in adultery illustrates this idea. Jesus was teaching in the Temple when the teachers of the Torah and the Pharisees brought a woman to him. These folks were very much aware of the verses in Scripture. But even knowing the verses, they were not in sync with God; they did not have a sense of the jazz of God's Word. Knowing that the law demanded that she be stoned to death, they asked Jesus what should be done.

Jesus understood the jazz aspect of Scripture. He was in sync with God, could feel the heart and pulse of God. He took his time in responding. The religious leaders, so intent on the verse, continued to demand an answer from him. Finally he spoke: "All right, stone her. But let those who have never sinned throw the first stones!" (verse 7) The crowd was stunned. What kind of answer was that! Slowly the teachers and Pharisees began to leave, and the woman was left standing before Jesus.

But that is not where the story ends. That is not the "jazz" part of the story, the part between the verses. The jazz part occurs when Jesus says, "Where are your accusers? Didn't even one of them condemn you?" The woman replied, "No, Lord"; then Jesus said, "Neither do I. Go and sin no more." (verses 10-11)

Yesterday, we talked about Scripture being the breath of God. The jazz metaphor enhances this understanding. When we read the Bible, we open ourselves to the movement of God's Spirit, the breath of God. We listen for God's voice between the verses. We strive not to be people of the verse, as the Pharisees were, but people of the breath, as Jesus was.

At one of the churches I served, there was a policy and procedure manual outlining how education ministries would be handled. It was a thorough manual with important policies to safeguard the children who participated in our ministries. However, as valuable as it was, in one section there was a policy prohibiting persons who were divorced from teaching Sunday school. Granted, divorce is a tragic event in the life of any family, wrecking havoc on adults and children alike. It is not a choice the church needs to advocate or endorse; yet, at the same time, it appears that in this particular policy, more attention was paid to the "verse" than to the breath of God between the verses. It is as if those who drafted that exacting policy knew the verse but didn't understand the jazz—that nothing can separate us from the love of God or exclude us from total and complete forgiveness in Jesus Christ. Better if our policy had been to recognize that we are all fallen creatures, sinful and in need of grace. Better to have become people of the breath by recognizing our own need of God's forgiveness and healing power and offering that same forgiveness and opportunity for healing to others.

Applying God's teaching to our daily lives can be a difficult thing. It will be even more difficult if we read God's Word without any connection to the movement of the Holy Spirit. In the movie *The Last Crusade* Indy prays before reading the diary, "May he who illuminated this, illuminate me." Each time we open the Bible that should be our prayer as well. May the one who illuminated this, illuminate me. We will remain persons of the verse unless we take the time necessary to hear God speaking to us between the verses. Moral ambiguity surrounds us more than ever. Issues like abortion, homosexuality, and divorce clamor for our attention, and the hedge we spoke of on Day One can at times seem indistinct. But if we are to make God the main thing, we must not only be aware of the verses in Scripture, we must be in tune with the jazz of Scripture —the voice of God, speaking between the verses.

Reflecting and Recording

Have you ever experienced someone who was a person of the verse rather than a person of the breath? If so, how did that experience feel?

Spend some time thinking about an event or situation in your life when it was easier to be a person of the verse rather than seeking to hear God's voice speaking between the verses.

*

Recall a time when you were a person of the breath, in sync with the heart and pulse of God. What were your feelings surrounding that situation or event? How did you feel in the aftermath?

During the Day

Be aware of opportunities to be a person of the breath as you relate to others today.

DAY FOUR: THE WORD OF GOD

I run the way of your commandments,
for you enlarge my understanding.
(Psalm 119:32, New Revised Standard Version*)*

Look back at the description of the scene in *Indiana Jones and the Last Crusade* on Day Two. What were the clues contained in the diary? "First, the breath of God, only the penitent man may pass. Second, the word of God, only in the footsteps of God will he succeed." Again, this scene offers a marvelous metaphor for Scripture: It is the word of God.

That kind of description—the word of God—can make some of us a bit uncomfortable, it sounds narrow and limiting. Recall our discussion on Day One. We often assume Scripture to be constraining rather than life giving; yet remembering that God has chosen to communicate with us *for our benefit* encourages us to move beyond our current ideological mindsets. In this way Scripture expands our perspective. The verse from Psalm 119 that began our reading today highlights this idea; when we seek to make God's Word a part of our daily lives, our understanding increases.

God's Word is a life-enlarging word, a word that moves us beyond the limits of our own point of view. Saying that the Bible confines us is like saying that God's Word is smaller than our word. Such a statement is a prime example of human pride and arrogance. Ashleigh Brilliant, a humorist of the seventies, wrote, "All I ask of life is a constant and exaggerated sense of my own importance." (James D. Berkley, "Eleven-gallon Head," *Leadership Weekly,* 10-3-02) That is at the heart of an understanding of God's Word as limiting—an exaggerated sense of our own importance. For how can it be that a human word, a human perception, could be larger than God's word, the very word that when uttered brought all of creation into being? Asserting such an overconfident idea might seem to me to evoke a response from God similar to the one Job received:

Where were you when I laid the foundations of the earth? Tell me, if you know so much. Do you know how its dimensions were determined and who did the surveying? What supports its foundations, and who laid its cornerstone as the morning stars sang together and all the angels shouted for joy? . . . But of course you know all this! For you were born before it was all created, and you are so very experienced!
(Job 38:4-7, 21; New Living Translation*)*

That our word could be more expansive than God's Word sounds strange because it is a misunderstanding. It is our word that is narrow and limiting. Bringing ourselves into alignment with God's Word opens our perspective and widens our understanding. Recall our discussion of the God-breathed nature of Scripture on Day Two and my experience with the bishop's devotional. Recognizing the Holy Spirit breathing in Scripture enabled me to be receptive to God's movement in my life in a new and different way, even as the Bible itself and the story it contained remained unchanged.

Understanding the Bible as God's powerful Word reinforces that receptivity. When we dispel an exaggerated sense of our own importance and become conscious of the limits of our own word, the narrowness of our own perspective, capabilities, and discernment, we are able to approach Scripture with a sense of awe and wonder, keenly aware of the expansiveness of God's Word and its ability to open us to new and deeper levels of faith and understanding.

Reflecting and Recording

Take some time to reflect on the ways your perspective might be narrower than God's perspective.

✳

Describe some of the ways we exaggerate our own importance, thinking that we have a broader, more enlightened perspective than God.

Why do you believe we think in this way?

During the Day

Be aware of times when you presume to have a broader perspective than God. Make note of the circumstances in which you are inclined to make this assumption.

DAY FIVE: ABSOLUTE TRUTH

*For I was hungry, and you fed me. I was thirsty, and you gave me a drink. I was a
stranger, and you invited me into your home. I was naked, and you gave me
clothing. I was sick, and you cared for me. I was in prison, and you visited me.
(Matthew 25:35-36, New Living Translation)*

Even as God's Word expands our perspective, we must proceed with caution
when coming to an understanding of the Bible as God's Word. Many of us have
been deeply hurt by those who would use Scripture as a hammer, thumping
others on the head and heart with "the Word of God." Preachers sometimes proclaim that the Bible is absolute truth, the implication being that therefore, they
themselves have absolute truth. Such proclamations would be less troublesome
if they did not so often result in this "absolute truth" being used to alienate, tear
down, and oppress. The deeper question raised by claims of possessing absolute
truth is how any human being could ever completely grasp absolute truth. Only
God can contain absolute truth. We are simply not big enough.

Mike Slaughter's gift of communication helps us once again by turning the
question around. Rather than wondering if we possess absolute truth, he asks,
Does absolute truth possess us? He asserts that if absolute truth possesses us, we
will not simply be people of the verse, quoting and memorizing and hammer-
ing the hearts and heads of others with words contained in Scripture. Instead
we will be people of the breath, *demonstrating* the power of God's Word in the
world. If absolute truth possesses us, others will know it because they will be
able to see it in our actions. The proof lies not in how much Scripture we know;
the proof lies in our actions toward people.

This is where we begin to move deeper into the process of making God the main thing, of incorporating God's word into our daily lives. Several years ago, the government in my small midwestern town enacted an ordinance that limited the display of a crèche on the lawn of our county courthouse. Each year since that ruling, there has been a controversy over the public display of the crèche. Over the years, numerous letters written by Christian folks have appeared in the newspaper expressing outrage at the secularization of this most important holiday. How dare the courts remove such a significant symbol? Yet each year I wonder where, in the metaphorical sense, is the crèche on the front lawn of these people's personal lives? How are they able to proclaim Christ as the "reason for the season" when their words are shrill and even hurtful?

We don't incorporate God's word into our daily life simply by our mastery of Scripture; God's word is incorporated into our lives through our commitment to being a channel of God's love in the world. In Matthew 25 Jesus tells us that in the end it will be the power of God's love expressed through our actions that carries the day, not our knowledge of Scripture.

"When did we ever see you hungry and feed you? Or thirsty and give you some-thing to drink? Or a stranger and show you hospitality? Or naked and give you clothing? When did we ever see you sick or in prison, and visit you?" And the King will tell them, "I assure you, when you did it to one of the least of these my brothers and sisters, you were doing it to me!"
(Matthew 25:37-40, New Living Translation)

God becomes the main thing, or as Slaughter says, absolute truth possesses us, when we begin to *live* God's word rather than simply *read* God's word. Yet this cannot be easily done alone; rather it is meant to be accomplished in community. Human beings have an incredible flair for rationalization. We have proven time and again that we are capable of making the Bible say whatever we want it to say. Thus, in my journey toward making God the main thing, I need the Christian community to help me understand God's Word and trans-fer it to my daily living; I need it to guard me against turning the gospel of Jesus Christ into the gospel of *me*. The community of faith, particularly a small group, provides us with sounding boards, giving us important confir-mation or significant words of caution as we seek to live out what we read in God's Word.

Reflecting and Recording

Reflect on a time when someone "thumped" you with Scripture. What was your response? How did it make you feel about God and God's Word?

✳

Describe some ways that you might begin to live God's Word rather than just reading it. How might the community of faith aid you in this process?

During the Day
Put at least one of your thoughts about living God's Word into action today.

DAY SIX: THE PATH OF GOD

Show me the path where I should walk, O Lord;
point out the right road for me to follow.
Lead me by your truth and teach me,
for you are the God who saves me.
All day long I put my hope in you.
(*Psalm 25:4-5,* New Living Translation*)*

Looking at the scene from *Indiana Jones and the Last Crusade* described on Day Two again furthers our understanding of Scripture and its import in making God the main thing in our lives. The third clue in the diary was, "the path of God, only in the leap from the lion's head will he prove his worth." Scripture is the path of God.

The imagery is significant. The Bible is not an end in itself. Scripture is the map, not the destination. It marks the path toward the purpose and future God has created for each one of us; and we must refer to it regularly if we are to reach our destination.

As my writing ministry has unfolded, I have begun speaking at more conferences and workshops beyond my local church. Recently I preached at Wheaton College in Wheaton, Illinois, at the invitation of the chaplain. When I agreed to preach, the chaplain indicated that his secretary would send additional information in preparation for my visit. As promised, a two-page letter arrived containing three additional pages of instructions about my visit. A wide variety of information covering all aspects of my visit was included—the schedule for the day, a description of the chapel service, directions to my hotel and to the college, a walking map of the campus and special points of interest. It was clear that the folks at Wheaton wanted to make sure that I got there and that I stayed there once I had arrived.

As considerate as the folks at Wheaton were, their kindness was just a reflection of ordinary human commitment—the politeness shown to any guest who may not know his or her way around unfamiliar territory. How much more do you think God loves us? God loves us so much that God was willing to become human and die—for each one of us. And God has given us a map, multiple pages of instructions and information—the Bible—to make sure we "get there."

Scripture, the map, is not the destination; and it may not always feel complete as we try to use it to move toward the destination God has created for us. In fact, we are told that there were many things that Jesus did and many God-events that people saw and experienced that are not even written down. But we are also told that there is enough written down, the map is detailed enough, to enable us to come to believe in Jesus Christ as God's means of salvation and restoration (John 20). As we come to believe, as our faith is strengthened, we are able to move God closer and closer to the center of our lives, trusting that God's Word will provide the instructions we need to reach our destination.

Toward the end of *Indiana Jones and the Last Crusade*, Indy must negotiate a series of life-threatening challenges as he gets closer and closer to finding the Holy Grail. At each challenge, remembering the clues in the diary saves him from certain death. Finally, he finds himself on a small ledge on the side of a cliff. In front of him is a huge chasm; on the other side is the pathway he needs. Below him is a seemingly bottomless abyss. There appears to be no way forward. He begins to panic even as he continues to recite the three clues from the diary —the breath of God, the word of God, the path of God. There does not seem to be any path.

"The path of God, only in the leap from the lion's head will he prove his worth." As he says these words, Indy realizes that he must act on faith; he must leap, trusting that the clues that have guided him thus far will continue to bear him along. He screws up all his courage and steps forward into the abyss. As he does, rather than falling into the chasm, he steps onto a stone bridge that miraculously appears beneath his outstretched foot, bearing the full force of his weight and carrying him safely to the other side.

There will be times when the path God has laid before us seems unclear. We may be uncertain about the destination toward which God is leading us. We may feel insecure about our future and God's purpose for us. Yet, even in the midst of uncertainty we must remind ourselves that everything we need to know has been given to us in the context of God's Word. Moving God to the center of our lives involves trusting that the clues that have guided us thus far will continue to bear us toward God's future. With that trust, we can step out in faith, confident that as we commit ourselves more and more to living out God's Word, a path will appear that will lead us in the right direction.

Reflecting and Recording

Have there been times when your path has seemed unclear? If so, describe that experience. Where did you turn for answers? How did you negotiate the ambiguity?

Write about a time when God's Word provided you with guidance in making a life decision. How did you feel as this experience unfolded?

During the Day

God spoke through the prophet Jeremiah, saying, "I know the plans I have for you. . . . They are plans for good and not for disaster, to give you a future and a hope." (Jeremiah 29:11, New Living Translation) Keep this passage in your mind as you go through your activities today. Remember that God uses God's Word as a means to reveal God's plan to you.

DAY SEVEN: THE BREATH, THE WORD, THE PATH

Stick with what you learned and believed, sure of the integrity of your teachers—why, you took in the sacred Scriptures with your mother's milk! There's nothing like the written Word of God for showing you the way to salvation through faith in Christ Jesus.
(2 Timothy 3:14-15, THE MESSAGE)

Today concludes the first week of our journey to strengthen our ability to live God's teachings and enhance the connection between faith and daily life. We have begun with Scripture—God's breath, God's word, God's path—in order for you to see the intimate relationship between God's self-communication and our ability to make God the main thing. Our God is not some abstract notion, a philosophical construct to be debated and discussed. Therefore, while academic debate over theology and philosophy can be meaningful, it will not lie at the very core of our efforts to make God the main thing. Our God is not a disinterested observer, a deity who created but then stepped back simply to watch as the drama unfolded. Therefore, making God the main thing is not about trying to make contact with some distant, unreachable cosmic being. Our God is a God who is intensely connected to all creation, who chose to reveal God's self through the divine drama of human history, culminating in God's self-revelation through Jesus Christ; and who continues to reveal God's self through Scripture, the dynamic, interactive, God-breathed Word of God through which each of us can find the path to our created purpose. Making this God the main thing, then, is about recognizing a vibrant power that is alive and already present, already close, already available for us.

We begin with Scripture because that is the place where we encounter this living God. It is the place where the breath of God can begin to move in our lives. There are many things that seek to be the main thing in our lives—money, materialism, greed; but the Bible asks, how will we benefit if we gain the whole world but lose our own souls in the process? (Mark 8:36) The media would place sex and the pursuit of pleasure at the center of our lives; but the Scripture says, "Don't you know that your body is the temple of the Holy Spirit, who lives in you and was given to you by God? You do not belong to yourself, for God bought you with a high price. So you must honor God with your body." (1 Corinthians 6:19-20, New Living Translation) Society urges us to focus on gaining power and prestige, but the Bible tells us that when God's kingdom comes, all those who seem to be important now will become the least important, and all those who are considered least here will become the greatest. (Mark 10:31)

We begin with Scripture because that is where we encounter the living God, but we also begin there because that is the means that God has chosen to show us the path to our future. It is our map, our blueprint for living—not just living in the physical sense of good health and well-being, but living in the deeper sense of abundant life, of living in tune with God's grace and purpose for our lives. Maxie Dunnam put it well when he said, "When our minds are open to understand the Scripture, our hearts are open to receive God's grace." That is what Scripture as the breath, word, and path of God are all about. But that is not all. He continues, "When our minds are open to understand the Scripture, our hearts are open to receive God's grace. When our hearts are open to receive God's grace, our wills are softened to do God's bidding." (Maxie D. Dunnam, "The Authority of Scripture: God's Breathed Word," sermon preached at Christ United Methodist Church, Memphis, Tennessee, Sunday, April 30, 2000)

Moving God to the center of our lives involves the experience of God's grace and the softening of our wills to do God's bidding. That is why beginning with Scripture is so important—because our faith begins with God's grace, which we encounter so vividly in Scripture, the record of God's movement of love toward us. The entire biblical witness is to the reality of God staying with us, through God's grace, pursuing us, loving us, desiring to restore us to the selves we were created to be, to bring us back into relationship with God. Connecting our faith with our daily lives involves the experience of God's grace, which softens our wills to do God's bidding. That softening shifts to strength as we increasingly take advantage of the opportunity to follow wherever it is that Christ leads us.

Reflecting and Recording

What cultural messages are jostling for a place at the center of your life? The desire for money? Prestige? Career advancement? A particular relationship? Your family?

How do you see your will softening as a result of experiencing God's grace? What do you believe the role of Scripture has been in that softening? How is this experience affecting you as you seek to make God the main thing in your life?

During the Day

Remain focused on Maxie Dunnam's words today: When our minds are open to understand the Scripture, our hearts are open to receive God's grace. When our hearts are open to receive God's grace, our wills are softened to do God's bidding.

Clip these words from the back of this workbook and put them in a prominent place.

GROUP MEETING FOR WEEK ONE

Introduction

During the six weeks together, you will receive the most meaning from the weekly group meetings if they reflect the experience of all the participants. What follows are suggestions that may be useful and help facilitate your time together as a group. Ideas are important, and we benefit when we wrestle with new ideas as well as with ideas with which we disagree. It is important, however, that the group meeting not become a debate about ideas. People, rather than ideas, should be emphasized—experiences, feelings, and meaning. Content is important; but its importance lies in how it applies to our individual lives, our relationship to God and others.

As the study progresses, the group will come to the place where all can share honestly and openly about what is happening in their lives. Arriving at this place of honest sharing will enhance the meaning of the experience. This does not mean sharing only the good or positive; it involves sharing the struggles, the difficulties, the negatives as well. This process of honest sharing is not easy; we deceive ourselves when we act as though it is. Growth requires effort. Do not be afraid to share your questions, reservations, and "dry periods" as well as that in which you find meaning.

Sharing Together

As you anticipate your group meeting, use these suggestions to prepare for discussion.

- Think about your experience with the workbook. What difficulties are you encountering? What are you finding most meaningful?
- Think about your experience of attending to or ignoring Scripture.
- Consider the assertion that the Bible is God's means of self-communication, that God is active in speaking to us through Scripture *now,* and that God's self-communication is *for our benefit.*
- Identify a time when Scripture touched you at an important point of need.
- Consider the descriptions of persons as either people of the verse or people of the breath. Which are you?
- Describe some of the ways you would like to begin living God's Word rather than just reading it. (See Reflecting and Recording, Day Five, page 35.) How might members of the group aid one another in this process?
- Think about and describe a time when your path seemed unclear and what you did to gain clarity.
- Consider a time when God's Word provided guidance in making a life decision.

Praying Together

Corporate prayer is one of the great blessings of Christian community; thus, each week the group is asked to pray together. There is power in communal prayer, and it is important that we include this dimension as we journey together.

It is also important that people feel comfortable and that no pressure be placed on anyone to pray aloud. God is infinitely able to hear our prayers even when our words are not spoken aloud. Silence, where thinking is centered and attention is focused, may provide our deepest periods of prayer. Verbal prayers, then, should be offered spontaneously as a person chooses to pray aloud—it is not always helpful to "go around the circle and pray when it is your turn."

What is happening in the meeting—the mood, the needs that are expressed, the timing—these are the things that should determine the direction for group prayer. There may be occasions when, as you share together, the need for prayer in that moment will become apparent. Here are some ideas to include in your group meeting prayer time.

- Think about the sharing that has taken place during the session. What personal needs or concerns came out of the sharing? Begin to speak these aloud with any person verbalizing a need or a concern that has been expressed. Do not hesitate to mention a concern that you may have picked up from another woman in the group. For example, "Mary isn't able to be with us this week because her son is in the hospital. Let's pray for her son and for her." It will be beneficial for each person to make notes of the concerns and needs that are expressed. Enter deliberately into a period of silence. The leader may verbalize each of these needs in turn, allowing for a brief period following each so that all might center their attention and focus their prayers on the person, need, or concern mentioned. All of this can be done in silence as each woman prays in her own way.
- Offer brief spontaneous verbal prayers. For example: (a) Thank God for the group and the opportunity to share with others in this study/learning/prayer experience. (b) Confess that we are all sinners in need of God's love and forgiveness, and ask God to open each of us to ourselves and to one another, to be honest in our sharing and genuine caring for one another, and to be open to receive truth as it comes from God.

- If you have an instant-developing camera, contact the leader of your group about bringing it and take a picture of each woman in the group. Turn the pictures facedown on a table and let each person take one. This is the woman for whom you will pray specifically this week. Before you go, take a few minutes to visit with the woman whose picture you chose, getting to know her better. Ask if there are things coming up in her life about which you might pray. If an instant camera is not available, write the name of each person in your group on a slip of paper and have each person draw a name.

Week Two:
What Faith We Have

DAY ONE: WHO IS THIS GOD?

*Now we look inside, and what we see is that anyone united with the Messiah gets
a fresh start, is created new. The old life is gone; a new life burgeons! . . .
We're speaking for Christ himself now: Become friends with God;
he's already a friend with you.
(2 Corinthians 5:17, 20; THE MESSAGE)*

As we discovered last week, making God the main thing in your life is more than
merely applying God's teachings to our lives as though they were advice from a self-
help manual. We must understand the importance of Scripture as God's dynamic
means of self-communication. What we discover in the Bible is not simply wise
counsel; it is the power of God to transform our lives. Being open to the transforming power of God requires not only that we value the authority of Scripture
as God's breathed Word, but that we develop an ongoing relationship with it.
That ongoing relationship, that desire to be connected intimately with Scripture,
is the channel through which God's transforming power flows. As I have con-
versed with other preachers and listened to various sermons, four elements have
emerged as needing to be at the forefront of our relationship with Scripture:
knowing the Bible, believing the Bible, praying the Bible, and *applying the Bible.*

Clearly, commitment to applying the Bible is one of the main goals of this
study. We desire to make God the main thing by strengthening the connection
between Scripture and our daily lives. This element of our relationship with
Scripture will thus follow us throughout these next weeks. While praying the
Bible will also be a part of our focus, for now I want to concentrate on the first
two elements, *knowing* and *believing.*

The title of this study, *Knowing God: Making God the Main Thing in My Life,* is intimately connected to the concept of knowing the Bible. As we discovered on our first day together, as Christians we believe the Bible is God's chosen means of self-communication. It is one of the ways in which God continues to reveal God's self to us in the midst of our current situation. Thus, coming to know God requires that we come to know Scripture. Knowing Scripture involves study. That is what you are involved in at this moment— the deliberate reading and reflecting on the Bible and other resources and intentional discussion with others. Knowing the Bible is also connected to our discussion on Day Four of Week One about Scripture being the Word of God. Coming to know the Bible is a mind-enlarging, life-enhancing process. Knowing the Bible is connected to our discussion of Scripture as the path of God on Day Six of Week One as well. The process of coming to know the Bible is the process of discerning the path that leads us toward God and God's plan for our lives.

Believing the Bible is the second element in developing an ongoing relationship with Scripture and thus opening ourselves to the transforming power of God. Believing the Bible is about faith. Therefore, it is crucial to explore our existing relationship with God and the nature of our faith. Who is this God that we believe in? How has our relationship with this God unfolded in our lives? Examining our faith relationship and its role in our lives is crucial if we are to continue to move forward on our spiritual journey. We begin with what faith we have and grow from there.

At the heart of our relationship with God should lay the experience of God's grace offered to us through Jesus Christ. This experience is the foundation of our faith and is one of the most significant elements that distinguish the Christian spiritual journey from all others. Recall our discussion last week at the end of Day Seven. Our faith begins with God's grace, God's loving activity in the world. Our God is a God who has sought us from the very beginning: creating us in love, desiring to live with us in love, then when we turned away, seeking to return us to that relationship of love.

From start to finish, the Bible witnesses to God's desire to be in loving relationship with us. The movement of God throughout the Old Testament— Creation, the covenants, the liberation of God's people from slavery—in all of it the divine movement of love is toward us. The New Testament culminates this loving movement in the person of Jesus Christ. Reflected in his birth, ministry, death, and resurrection is God's desire to stay with us, to woo us, to love us, to restore us to our created image and bring us back into loving relationship.

Believing the Bible starts with faith in this God, a God who will allow nothing to separate us from God's love, a God who creates us and ransoms us and calls us by name. A God who promises never to abandon or forsake us, saying, "When you go through deep waters and great trouble, I will be with you. When you go through rivers of difficulty, you will not drown! When you walk through the fire of oppression, you will not be burned up; the flames will not consume you. For I am the LORD, your God, the Holy One of Israel, your Savior." (Isaiah 43:2-3, New Living Translation) This, and no other, is the God whom we desire to make the main thing in our lives.

Reflecting and Recording

Reflect on your current understanding and experience of God—the ways in which you have felt God's movement of love toward you.

✳

In what ways has your experience been similar to or different from the biblical witness of God seeking to stay with us, woo us, love us, restore us to our created image, and bring us back into loving relationship?

During the Day

Be aware of the ways God is moving toward you—through the people you may encounter today, the circumstances in which you may find yourself, the activities you undertake.

DAY TWO: OUR POINT OF DEPARTURE

It wasn't so long ago that you were mired in that old stagnant life of sin. You let the world, which doesn't know the first thing about living, tell you how to live. You filled your lungs with polluted unbelief, and then exhaled disobedience. We all did it, all of us doing what we felt like doing, when we felt like doing it, all of us in the same boat. It's a wonder God didn't lose his temper and do away with the whole lot of us.
(Ephesians 2:1-3, THE MESSAGE)

Yesterday, we began to explore the nature of our faith, asking who this God is that we believe in. We continue that exploration by asking, How has our relationship with this God unfolded in our lives? Where are we on our journey of faith? To better understand our relationship with God and to locate ourselves on our spiritual journey, we must start at the beginning, at our point of departure.

The relationship between God and humanity revealed in Scripture and confirmed by experience is one of covenant making and keeping on God's part and covenant making and breaking on our part. Our God is a God who created each of us as one whole, good self, a God who desires to be in relationship with us and again and again makes covenants with us to seal that relationship. Because God wanted this relationship to be free, rather than one of coercion, manipulation, or force, God provided us with an independent will and granted us the freedom to choose. Somewhere along the way, however, something happened to that good, whole self and to our relationship with God. Our wholeness became fragmented and our relationships with God and one another estranged. In the marred exercise of our wills, we became supremely vulnerable and responsive to the power of evil.

48

This predicament of estrangement and a lack of wholeness is what we have traditionally referred to as sin. It is the conflict that seems to rage within each of us, the good selves we were created to be battling against the evil that lies all around us. Paul described it this way:

No matter which way I turn, I can't make myself do right. I want to, but I can't. When I want to do good, I don't. And when I try not to do wrong, I do it anyway. (Romans 7:18-19, New Living Translation)

Within each of us lies the desire to follow the good yet an intense susceptibility to the allure of the evil that surrounds us. This inner conflict is our point of departure. It is where we begin as we explore our relationship with God.

Identifying this conflict should not discourage us; it is simply an objective fact, but it is crucial for us to recognize if we are to understand and deepen our relationship with God. At the same time we comprehend the objective fact of our sin, we also remember that we belong to God, who created each of us as one good, whole self, and who has been seeking to be in relationship with us ever since. In a book I co-authored with Maxie Dunnam, *The Workbook on Virtues and the Fruit of the Spirit*, we put it this way:

Each of us is a unique, unrepeatable miracle of God. God wants each of us to recognize that we belong to God. God desires our free choosing of relationship, just as God freely chose to create us in the first place.
(The Workbook on Virtues and the Fruit of the Spirit, *Upper Room Books, 1998; page 15)*

Realizing that even in the midst of our inner conflict we have been given the freedom to choose—to move toward God and the good selves we were created to be, or to move in greater sync with the evil that surrounds us—should be an emboldening experience. We do not have to remain at the beginning. Our situation of inner conflict is actually our *point of departure*, not our destination. We do not have to succumb to our inner responsiveness to evil. Rather we can choose to deepen our relationship with God, move God toward the center of our lives and us closer to becoming the good selves God created us to be.

Reflecting and Recording

Spend a few minutes reflecting on our inner conflict between good and evil as the point of departure for our spiritual journey.

What role has the recognition of this conflict played in your spiritual journey thus far?

During the Day

Be aware of the ways in which good and evil pull at you as you make various choices today. Be particularly alert to the subtle differences.

DAY THREE: THE FIRST STEP ON THE JOURNEY

When we were utterly helpless, Christ came at just the right time and died for us sinners. Now, no one is likely to die for a good person, though someone might be willing to die for a person who is especially good. But God showed his great love for us by sending Christ to die for us while we were still sinners. And since we have been made right in God's sight by the blood of Christ, he will certainly save us from God's judgment. For since we were restored to friendship with God by the death of his Son while we were still his enemies, we will certainly be delivered from eternal punishment by his life. So now we can rejoice in our wonderful new relationship with God—all because of what our Lord Jesus Christ has done for us in making us friends of God.
(Romans 5:6-11, New Living Translation*)*

We continue to explore the nature of our faith by looking again at where we are on our journey of faith and how our relationship with God has unfolded in our lives. We have discovered the point of departure in our divine-human relationship—that inner conflict between the good selves we were created to be and the allure of evil around us. Moving forward from that point involves the realization that we are not alone in resolving that conflict. In fact, if left to our own devices, we would be unable to resolve that conflict. If, in aspiring to make God the main thing and connect Scripture to our daily lives we believe that all we need to do is follow the teachings found in the Bible, we will be sorely disappointed. That is what Paul was trying to warn us about when he wrote, "I love God's law with all my heart. But there is another law at work within me that is at war with my mind. This law wins the fight and makes me a slave to the sin

51

that is still within me." (Romans 7:22-23, New Living Translation) Our internal battle is not one we are able to win on our own power. Knowing God's law, understanding God's teachings, only serve to make us aware of how incapable we are to keep them.

The good news is that we do not have to fight this battle alone. The very God that desires to be in relationship with us is the God who makes that relationship possible by providing the resolution to our inner conflict. That resolution is Jesus Christ, who through his death and resurrection conquered the power of evil in the world. Scripture is unambiguous about this: Evil has been overcome. Our hope, as we seek to make God the main thing, is not just hearing that message but experiencing that victory ourselves. It is in grasping that God's grace is more powerful than our sin. It is in recognizing that our relationship with God is one of friendship—friendship that has been created because God put God's love on the line in becoming human in Jesus, fully living, sacrificially dying, and triumphantly rising for us.

Experiencing God's grace, restoring our friendship with God, begins when we recognize our sinfulness, earnestly repent, and accept the forgiveness God offers us through Jesus Christ. The grace we experience, referred to as justifying grace, is the redemptive, healing, recreating love of God. It is a gift from God that we receive not because we deserve it, or have earned it, but because God freely gives it. It is a radical love for us, a love that is more powerful than sin, that reconciles our relationship, and "makes us right" with God. When we accept that grace, we experience "justification"; God wipes the slate of our lives clean, and we are able to move forward on our spiritual journey empowered by God's love.

A sense of God's grace is a critical element in knowing God and making God the main thing in our lives. Without an awareness of grace, our goal of bridging the gap between Scripture and our daily lives will at best become merely an exercise in rule following an empty legalism. At its worst it will become a desperate means of earning God's love and friendship, an experience destined for discouragement when we fail, and fear of the consequences of that failure. Grace must lie at the heart of our relationship with God. It is the foundation for all else, and only in genuinely experiencing it will we be able to move God to the center of our lives in a full and life-sustaining way.

Reflecting and Recording

Think about your relationship with God at this moment. Write some of the words you would use to describe that relationship.

As you have sought to make God the main thing, what have been your motivators in the past? Fear? The desire to please? Gratitude? Record your thoughts.

Reflect on your experience of God's grace. Remember that our Christian experience is a process. Justifying grace comes to us when we claim the fact that we are forgiven, accepted by God as we are, and loved unconditionally. Make some notes about your experience. What has happened in your life in conjunction with that experience? What were your feelings? What action did you take in response? Make notes to get that experience of God's justifying grace firmly in your mind.

During the Day

As you go about your daily activity today, live joyfully, knowing that your relationship with God is one of friendship—friendship that has been created because God put God's love on the line in becoming human in Jesus, fully living, sacrificially dying, and triumphantly rising for you.

DAY FOUR: OUR GIGANTIC SECRET

Always be full of joy in the Lord. I say it again—rejoice!
(Philippians 4:4, New Living Translation*)*

For some of us the last few days may have been a time to revisit the founda-tions of our faith; for others, it may have been a time of new insights. For all of us, rehearsing the essentials of the Christian faith ought to put us in a joyous mood; in fact, Christians ought to be the most joyful people on the planet. For some reason, however, we're not—or at least we don't appear to be. Rather than joy being our best-known attribute, it is our best-kept secret. I bring this up at this point in our journey together because at its most basic level, that is what this study is all about—joy. In coming to know God, we come to know the deep, abiding joy of being in relationship with a God who accepts us as we are and pledges never to abandon us. The by-product of making this God the main thing in our lives is the overflowing joy of being received even when we are not worthy, of being forgiven and restored to a life buoyed by the redemptive, heal-ing, recreating love of God.

Joy is at the heart of our faith. Last week on Day Three, we talked about understanding the "jazz" of Scripture. Jazz is cool, not always because of the notes, but because of the space between the notes. So it is with joy. The joy that lies at the heart of our faith comes not when we simply know the verses of Scripture but when we get in tune with what God is saying between the verses.

In *The Workbook on Virtues and the Fruit of the Spirit,* a story appears about Mark Twain who cut himself shaving and burst forth with a torrent of swearing and vulgar language. His wife heard him, was mortified, and hoped to shame him into better behavior—so she repeated back to him, word for word, his tirade. When she finished, he smiled at her and said, "You have the words, my dear, but I'm afraid you'll never master the tune."

Joy is the best-kept secret of Christians because we have the words but have not yet mastered the tune. We do not yet have a grasp on the "jazz" of our faith. We remain people of the verse instead of people of the breath. Joy is the tune of our faith. At each step of our spiritual journey we need to bring the words and the tune together, immersing ourselves in the stream of love and joy that flows from God.

One of the best ways to do this is to contemplate more seriously the fact of our salvation. The last two days have focused on that salvation experience, the recognition of our sinfulness and acceptance of the gift of God's grace that heals us; yet all too often that experience fades into the background as we travel farther along in our faith. The farther we get from the reality of our salvation, it seems, the less visible our joy becomes.

There is a deep connection between the reality of our salvation and the depth of our joy. To truly understand our salvation requires a true understanding of the intensity of our sin. The depth of our joy will be in direct proportion to the depth of our sorrow for our sin.

Scripture vividly illustrates this truth. In story after story, those most grateful, those most joyful in their newfound relationship with Jesus Christ, are those whose need was the greatest—the woman who anointed Jesus with oil, blind Bartimaeus, Zacchaeus. The most joy-filled letter Paul ever wrote was written from prison. He tells the Philippians to rejoice and always be full of joy.

Martin Luther said that we will have as much joy and laughter in life as we have faith in God. That is because the joy we experience through our relationship with God is not connected to our circumstances. It is deeper than that. It is grounded in the reality of our salvation and rooted in commitment and trust that God will take care of us. In Paul's Letter to the Philippians he says the "same God who takes care of me will supply all your needs from his glorious riches, which have been given to us in Christ Jesus." (Philippians 4:19, New Living Translation)

The biggest enemy of joy in our lives is self-pity. It separates us from the stream of love and joy that flows from God because it dislodges God from the center of our being and focuses us entirely on ourselves as the center of the universe. Elijah is a prime example of this. God had cared for him throughout his life and ministry. God had kept it from raining when Elijah asked for no rain and had used ravens to bring him food for an entire year. God had provided a widow to hide him from his enemies and sent fire to Elijah's altar when the priests of Baal were unable to create even a spark. Yet, despite all this, when confronted with the prospect of facing Jezebel's soldiers, Elijah was filled with self-pity, sure that God had abandoned him. The truth that is often difficult for us to accept is that God does not always work in the way we would like God to work. A companion truth, which is actually even more important, is that just because God does not work the way we would like does not mean God is not working. Our joy comes not in the *way* God works; our joy comes in the confidence and trust *that* God works.

Committing ourselves to making God the main thing is not meant to be drudgery. It is not meant to be a joyless experience of grim obligation. Moving God to the center of our lives is a process filled with the kind of immense and deep-seated joy that comes when we are aware of the reality of our salvation and trust that God will stick with us and care for us come what may. When we consistently make the connection between faith and daily living, that joy becomes visible and the possibilities arise for joy to become our best-known attribute rather than our gigantic secret.

Reflecting and Recording

Reflect on your feelings about the connection between sin and salvation, about your depth of sorrow for your sin and your joy in your salvation. How deep are these feelings?

*

How might self-pity be blocking you from the stream of love and joy that flow from God?

List three things you might do to increase your joy.

During the Day

Implement at least one of those three things today.

DAY FIVE: WHO AM I?

Do not act a part in public, keep watch over your lips.
(Ecclesiasticus 1:29, THE NEW JERUSALEM BIBLE)

Understanding the joyous nature of our faith involves not only understanding who God is and the characteristics of our relationship with God, it involves discovering who we are as well. As our understanding of ourselves increases, so does our ability to be in meaningful relationship with God and to make God the center of our lives. Discerning who we really are might seem like an easy task; however it can often be difficult for women, as society has numerous expectations regarding the roles women are to play in our culture. Rather than aiding us in discovering our authentic selves, these roles actually encourage an external rather than internal focus. Instead of moving us closer to answering "Who am I?" these roles obstruct our ability to understand ourselves and enslave us to the expectations others have of the particular role we have taken on.

Self-discovery can be a difficult process for women because it requires introspection and self-exploration. Society's expectations for the wide variety of women's roles are fairly well known; therefore, it often takes little effort to follow the basic script laid out for us. Focusing on ourselves rather than on our roles takes a great deal more effort, and we have not always been encouraged to undertake that effort. An underlying message of society, and even the church, is that a woman's effort toward self-knowledge is selfish or self-indulgent. This message often leads us to confuse the acknowledgment of the self with preoccupation with the self. Scripture has sometimes contributed to this misconception. Paul's explanation, "Our old sinful selves were crucified with Christ"

(Romans 6:6, New Living Translation) seems to imply that the self is not to be discovered or recognized, but eradicated. Again in Galatians, he describes the experience of God's grace: "I have been crucified with Christ. I myself no longer live, but Christ lives in me." (Galatians 2:19-20, New Living Translation)

It is easy to believe that we are to do away with ourselves completely. Yet self-discovery is crucial if we are to connect faith to our daily lives. This is one of the points I sought to make in *The Christ-Centered Women: Finding Balance in a World of Extremes:* "Without a sense of who we are as persons, we will never be able to discover who we are in relation to God or those around us." (*The Christ-Centered Women: Finding Balance in a World of Extremes,* Upper Room Books, 2000; page 57) Growing in our knowledge of God and moving God to the center of our lives involves not only effort that focuses on God, it involves effort that focuses on discovering our authentic selves as well.

Laurie Beth Jones is a successful writer, speaker, and consultant who has done a great deal of work in the business world. In that environment, she often finds herself in business suits; but in her book *Jesus in Blue Jeans: A Practical Guide to Everyday Spirituality,* she admits that she is most comfortable in much more casual attire. She tells the story of walking through an old flea market-type store in New Mexico. She had come to the store immediately after working with her horses and had not bothered to change out of her old hat, blue jeans, and muddy boots. As she was wandering through the aisle, a voice called out, "Hey—are you for real?" Not knowing exactly where the voice had come from, she turned and asked, "Excuse me?" The voice replied, "I said, are you really like how you're dressed, or is that just for show?" "Oh, this is me, all right," she laughed as she turned toward the sound of the voice. Out of a back room walked a very old lady, holding up an extraordinary antique Mexican bridle. "I've been saving this for someone who could appreciate it," the woman said as she carefully handed Laurie Beth her treasure. "I figured you might be for real." Laurie Beth concludes her story with these words, "Authentic. Made by hand. Certified by the Creator. One of a kind. . . . God created our authenticity. Why do we then struggle so much to be like others?" (Laurie Beth Jones, *Jesus in Blue Jeans: A Practical Guide to Everyday Spirituality;* Hyperion, 1997; pages 248–49)

God desires to be in relationship with us. God desires to make God's self known to us. As we seek to make God the main thing in our lives, we must follow Laurie Beth Jones's suggestion: Listen for God's voice calling to us, "Hey, are you for real? Are you really like you're dressed or is that outfit just for show? Because if you're for real, I will bring out my treasures to share with you." (page 248)

Reflecting and Recording

What roles are you currently playing? Are these roles enabling you to be "for real" or are they just for show?

Spend some time reflecting on the ways you have experienced being enslaved to the expectations others have of a particular role you have taken on.

*

Turn now to your authentic self. Recall an experience that brought out your authentic self.

*

What do you feel is the value of seeking authenticity in your relationship with God? How do you feel coming before God with your authentic self would enable you to connect your faith more strongly to your daily life?

During the Day

Be aware of the various roles you have accepted. Are you dressing and acting like who you want to be?

DAY SIX: I AM KIM

*But now thus says the L*ORD*,*
he who created you, O Jacob,
he who formed you, O Israel:
Do not fear, for I have redeemed you;
I have called you by name, you are mine.
(Isaiah 43:1, New Revised Standard Version*)*

I frequently lead workshops around the country on my book, *The Christ-Centered Woman.* There are many points of meaning for women in this book, but time and again they will focus on chapter four—"The Search for Our Center: Discovering Who We Are." This chapter looks at the importance of "naming" ourselves before God. Naming is an important part of understanding who we are. Our names identify us in relation to other people—Mrs. Reisman identifies me as the wife of John, the mother of Nathan, Maggie, and Hannah. My maiden name, Dunnam, identifies me as the daughter of Maxie and Jerry, the sister of Kerry and Kevin. These relationships are important; they are part of what has shaped and continues to shape me as an individual. My given name, Kimberly Lynn, on the other hand, does not identify me in relation to other people; rather it points more closely to who I am in my innermost being. Granted, there may be other Kimberly Lynn's in the world; but none are quite like me, with my fingerprints, my DNA, my God-created authenticity. The relationship that God desires to have with us is not a generic, one-size-fits-all relationship. It is a relationship in which God calls us by name and claims us as God's own. Yesterday I closed by focusing on God's question, "Are you for real?"

Naming ourselves before God is the way in which we answer that question. It is the way in which we say, "Yes God, I'm for real—this is me. I am Kim."

This naming process is not simply the practice of identifying ourselves; it is also the recognition that God is not waiting for us to be perfect. God desires for us to bring to our relationship with God whatever it is we are experiencing— the depth of our pain and confusion, the height of our joy and delight. So when we name ourselves before God, we are naming our *real* selves, not the selves we think we *should* be but the selves we actually are.

Naming ourselves before God, being "for real," enables us to be more aware of who we are at that particular time in our lives; but God does not stop with that experience. God uses that naming process to make it possible for us to discover the person God desires for us to become. Being "for real" opens us to God's *renaming* activity in our lives. That was the turning point in Jacob's life. After having grappled with God he received a new name: " 'Your name will no longer be Jacob,' the man told him. 'It is now Israel, because you have struggled with both God and men and have won.' " (Genesis 32:28, New Living Translation) In that moment, Jacob became the man God intended him to be. No longer Jacob the supplanter, the one who had unseated his brother Esau from his place as firstborn, now he was Israel, one who had power with God.

Jesus' baptism marked the beginning of his ministry. Until that time, people viewed him as any ordinary carpenter. For some, he may even have been seen as Joseph's "illegitimate" son. Yet, at his baptism, God announced to everyone that to see Jesus in this way was not to see him as God saw him. For God saw Jesus as beloved son (Mark 1:11).

God never sees us in the same way that we see ourselves. Nor does God see us as the world sees us. We may see ourselves as unacceptable, or maybe just exceedingly ordinary; the world may see us that way as well. But God never sees us as mundane, never as unacceptable. The person God sees is unique and loved and always named as a beloved child.

For us to successfully bridge the gap between faith and our daily lives, we must find the intersection between our genuine knowledge of ourselves that is reflected in our own naming and God's knowledge and renaming of us as God sees us. It is in that intersection that we will discover the person God intends us to be, the person God sees: a woman with unique gifts, a woman loved and cared for simply because she *is*. Discovering that person paves the way for a life lived in sync with God and God's intentions for our future.

Reflecting and Recording

How do you need to name yourself before God today? Angry? Heartbroken? Thankful? Contrite? Make notes to bring those feelings and the reasons behind them clearly into focus.

Take some time to come before God with whatever it is you are feeling in this moment—with your authentic self.

✳

Now spend some time in silence, opening yourself to God's renaming of you as the person God sees—beloved child.

✳

During the Day

As you go through your activities today, guard against seeing yourself through the world's eyes, or even through your own eyes. Be aware of your unique place as a child of God. Remember, God has called you by name; you belong to God.

DAY SEVEN: WHAT FAITH WE HAVE

I want you woven into a tapestry of love, in touch with everything there is to know of God. Then you will have minds confident and at rest, focused on Christ, God's great mystery. All the richest treasures of wisdom and knowledge are embedded in that mystery and nowhere else. And we've been shown the mystery! (Colossians 2:6-7, THE MESSAGE)

For some of you, this week may have been a review of truths that you have known and experienced for many years. For others, it may have been an exploration of entirely new territory, or perhaps terrain you have entered but are only just beginning to navigate. Regardless of where you find yourself, bringing to mind the basics of our faith (who God is, our point of departure, our first steps of faith) is an important process. We must always guard against two things: taking our faith for granted so that it becomes nothing more than window dressing for our lives, and misunderstanding the details of our faith so that we miss out on the depth of meaning that comes when we experience the great truths of God's love. Rehearsing the foundations of our faith guards us against both of those pitfalls and enables us to live in joy, "woven into a tapestry of love, in touch with everything there is to know about God." (Colossians 2:6, *THE MESSAGE*)

Guarding against those pitfalls is what Moses was trying to do when he spoke to the Israelites:

Keep these words that I am commanding you today in your heart. Recite them to your children and talk about them when you are at home and when you are away, when you lie down and when you rise. Bind them as a sign on your hand,

fix them as an emblem on your forehead, and write them on the doorposts
of your house and on your gates.
(Deuteronomy 6:6-9, New Revised Standard Version*)*

Our faith will never become relevant to our daily lives if we are not aware of what that faith is all about. We will never successfully make connections between our faith and the details of our lives if the tenets of that faith have grown so dim that they are no longer meaningful for us. Our faith is something we must rehearse again and again in order to keep it at the center of our lives.

Joshua echoed this commitment. The Israelites had entered the Promised Land and were beginning to settle there. They were settling into the life of a free people with their own land. Joshua reminded them of God's words and how they should begin their new life:

I gave you land you had not worked for, and I gave you cities you did not build—
the cities in which you are now living. I gave you vineyards and olive groves
for food, though you did not plant them. "So honor the LORD *and serve him*
wholeheartedly . . . choose today whom you will serve . . .
as for me and my family, we will serve the Lord."
(Joshua 24:13-15, New Living Translation*)*

Rehearsing our faith keeps it at the center of our lives. It reminds us where we have come from so that we will be able to see more clearly where we are in the present, to recognize what faith we have right now. Each day that we seek to make connections between our faith and the life that is unfolding around us, each time we come before God with our authentic selves, we do so with whatever faith we have at that moment. When we have a real sense of the foundations of our faith, we recognize that God receives us with what faith we have, loves us and accepts us, and in renaming us commits God's self to moving us from wherever we are to wherever God intends for us to be. In this way, we can experience the joy of being a tapestry of love, in touch with everything there is to know of God.

Reflecting and Recording

Take some time to reflect on your spiritual journey thus far. Start at the beginning of your faith walk and list the highlights that have marked your spiritual experience up to the present. Make notes to clearly bring these memories before you.

＊

How might you begin, or continue, rehearsing your faith in order to keep it at the center of your life?

I believe that when we have a real sense of the foundations of our faith, we are able to recognize that God receives us with the faith that we have, loves us and accepts us, and, in renaming us, commits God's self to moving us from wherever we are in the present to wherever God intends for us to be. Where do you see yourself at this point on your journey of faith? Where do you see God leading you?

During the Day
Take the time today to rehearse your faith and open yourself to God's leading.

GROUP MEETING FOR WEEK TWO

Introduction

Groups such as this involve a covenant relationship. Your benefit will be greatest through the keeping of daily disciplined study and faithful attendance at these weekly meetings. Don't feel guilty if your commitments necessitate missing a day in the workbook or be discouraged if your daily devotional time is not always adequate. Share those challenges with the group. Such sharing opens us to the opportunity to learn about ourselves. We may discover, for instance, that the content of a particular day was troublesome because of what it required or what it revealed about us. Our hesitation may have stemmed from an unconscious fear of dealing with the material. Patience is crucial—spiritual growth does not happen overnight. Recognize that God is working within you one step at a time and thus be open to what God may be seeking to teach you.

The spiritual growth we hope to experience during this time of study depends, in part, on group participation, so share as openly and honestly as you can. Listen to what others are saying; sometimes the meaning God intends for us to receive lies beyond the surface of their words. Only through attentive listening will we benefit. Participating in a sensitive fashion is important. When we pick up feelings as others share, it is important to respond immediately. As we discussed at the end of last week, if a need or concern is expressed, it may be appropriate for the leader to ask the group to enter into a brief period of special prayer for the persons or concerns revealed. Group members should not depend on the leader for this kind of sensitivity, because the leader may not always be aware. Each woman should feel free, regardless of who has taken a leadership responsibility, to ask the group to join in special prayer. You may all pray silently, or one person may wish to lead the group in prayer. Remember, you have a contribution to make to the group. Something that appears trivial or unimportant to you may be exactly what another woman in the group needs to hear. Being profound is not the goal, rather simply sharing our experience.

Sharing Together

As you prepare for your group meeting:
- Reflect on the most meaningful or the most difficult day in this week's workbook adventure. What made it so?
- Spend a few minutes thinking about what role your inner conflict has played in your spiritual journey.
- Reflect on the connection between your sorrow for sin and the depth of your joy.
- Remind yourself of your list of things that would increase your joy. (See Reflecting and Recording, Day Four, page 57.) Were you able to implement any of these ideas? Why or why not?
- Think about your feelings about the roles you play in life. Are they for real? Are they enslaving?

Praying Together

A commitment to pray for one another by name each day will dramatically enhance the effectiveness of the group and the quality of relationships that develop. One of the suggestions at the close of Week One was to take pictures of one another. If you have those pictures, use them again this week by putting them facedown on a table and letting each person select a picture. The woman chosen will be the focus of special prayer for the week. Bring the photos back next week, shuffle them, and draw again. Continue this throughout your pilgrimage together. Looking at a woman's picture as you pray for her will add meaning. Having her picture will also remind you that you are to give special prayer attention to her during the week.

Here are additional suggestions for your group prayer time:
- Review some of the sharing that has taken place during your time together. Begin praying by allowing each woman to mention any special needs she wishes to share with the entire group. A good pattern is to ask for a period of prayer after each need is mentioned. This may be silent prayer by the entire group, or someone may offer a brief two- or three-sentence verbal prayer.

• The Lord's Prayer links us with Christians of all time and in all places in universal praise, confession, thanksgiving, and intercession. Use this great prayer as a way to close your time together.

Week Three:
Shaping the Invisible

DAY ONE: THE RIGHT CONNECTIONS

God wanted them to look for him and perhaps search all around for him and find him, though he is not far from any of us: "We live in him. We walk in him. We are in him." Some of your own poets have said: "For we are his children." (Acts 17:27-28, New Century Version)

At the beginning of Week Two I mentioned four elements involved in our relationship with Scripture—knowing the Bible, believing the Bible, praying the Bible, and applying the Bible. We have discussed knowing and believing the Bible, and committing ourselves to applying the Bible is an ongoing goal of our time together. Now we turn to praying the Bible.

Currently, in our culture, there is little difference between the attitudes and behaviors of people within the church and those outside of it. George Barna, a leading authority on societal trends and religion, has been instrumental in highlighting the discrepancy between what Christians say they believe and how they actually behave. Whether it is lying, cheating, or even divorce, there is little measurable difference between Christians and non-Christians. This bespeaks, among other things, a tremendous lack of spiritual power in our lives. We seem to be disconnected from the source of spiritual power that would enable us to fully live out our faith. For many people this lack of spiritual power translates into a sense of emptiness, a longing for something more. Yet, rather than turning toward what could be our greatest source of power—God—we try to fill that emptiness with other things. Some of these things are ordinary outlets: our jobs, the wide variety of activities that so often fill our daily lives, entertainment. Other outlets are more harmful: unhealthy relationships, alcohol or substance abuse. In all of this searching there is clearly a desire for something beyond ourselves—we want to be connected to *something*; often we are just not sure what. That could be part of what prompted you to begin this study—that bit of longing for your faith to become more solidly connected, to become something more, something larger than you.

Do you remember the Bethlehem millennial celebration? To herald the 21st century, the city of Bethlehem, the birthplace of Jesus, held a tremendous celebration with fireworks and the release of "millennial birds." It sounds like a stirring moment, rich with symbolism. As the new millennium is ushered in, birds are released as a sign of our collective hope for peace. Yet the reality of that moment was far different. As the birds were released, fireworks were exploding and in the chaos of the noise and flashing light, rather than flying peacefully away as a flock, the birds became confused and frightened and flew helter-skelter all around the square, never really going anywhere.

What a great metaphor for our human condition. We flap around in our lives, confused and sometimes frightened, never completely comfortable with where we are flying. It is as though the connections are not right. That is what happened to the birds. Their connections were not right. It was nighttime, not the normal time for these birds to be flying. There were explosions going off all around them. They did not connect booming fireworks with safety and flying; instead they connected them to danger and fear. The connections were all wrong.

While I have ten years of ministry experience, I still consider myself more of a learner than a teacher. I depend on others for guidance, insight, and mentoring. As I reflect on that process, one thing has become clear from the lives of all those to whom I have turned for guidance: *spiritual discipline* is crucial. Some folks have mentored me in preaching, others in writing, others in pastoral leadership, each according to his or her gift. In all, however, there is a thread of commonality, regardless of their particular strength in ministry. That commonality is spiritual discipline, rooted in prayer.

Spiritual discipline grounded in prayer is the source of our connection to God. It is a primary means through which our emptiness is filled, and we experience the right connections that enable us to fly without confusion and fear. Without the attention to our interior selves that comes through prayer, we will be unable to know God or to make God the main thing in our lives. We will continue to live without the spiritual power to differentiate ourselves from those who do not share our faith. Thus, as we attempt to forge connections between our faith and our daily lives, committing ourselves to regular devotional and prayer time is an essential step.

Reflecting and Recording

How do you feel your life is differentiated from those who do not share your faith?

Spend some time reflecting on your current practice of prayer and other spiritual disciplines. How often do you take time to pray? Is it a regular practice? If not, what might you do to enhance this element of your spiritual life and forge connections that will enable you to fly without confusion and fear?

During the Day

Take a few extra minutes this morning to center yourself on God and the power available to you through prayer. Pray that God's Spirit might enervate you, strengthening you and enabling you to live out your faith in whatever circumstances you find yourself today.

DAY TWO: OUTSTRETCHED HANDS, INCHES APART

It is actually best for you that I go away, because if I don't, the Counselor won't come. If I do go away, he will come because I will send him to you.
(John 16:7, New Living Translation*)*

My 11-year-old daughter, Hannah, recently mastered throwing an M&M up into the air and catching it in her mouth. She was quite proud of her accomplishment and wanted me to see it. As you might expect, each time she tried in my presence, she missed; but no sooner had I left the room than she was successful once again. Hannah's experience illustrates a basic human truth: Only on rare occasions are we able to perform at our best in the presence of those who are most important to us. Our young children throw tantrums when we drop them off at preschool; yet they are fine the minute we leave the room. Even the disciples were not spared this unpleasant reality—none of the miracles they were able to perform in their ministries took place in Jesus' presence. It was only when he sent them out, and then again after he had left, that they were able to rise to the occasion. The dilemma for Christians, particularly as we seek to make connections between our faith and our daily lives, is that our God has, in a very mysterious sense, "gone away," while we remain to rise to the occasion.

Certainly we have been blessed with the power of the Holy Spirit, our Counselor, the one whom Jesus promised to send to us when he went away. Yet in a real way we can feel alone, disconnected. Michelangelo's famous depiction of Creation on the ceiling of the Sistine Chapel is a magnificent illustration of this feeling. God's hand stretches toward Adam, while Adam's hand extends back toward God—outstretched hands, with only inches to separate the fingers. How like our relationship with God: so close and yet so far away.

Our commitments can seem overwhelming; the hectic pace of our lives can leave us feeling chaotic and frazzled. The few inches that separate our fingers from God's fingers can seem more like a huge gulf. It can be easy to ask, "Why? Why would Jesus leave us if he cared for us so much? Why must we be left on our own to make the connection between our faith and daily life?" The answer can be more easily understood by looking at the disciples. While Jesus remained in human form, the possibility remained that the disciples' faith would be grounded not within their hearts but on the concrete confirmation of their senses. They could have faith because Jesus was *tangible*; they could see him and touch him; they could eat with him and hear him speak.

While Jesus was on earth, the disciples were just that—disciples, followers, students. Only after Jesus left them did they become apostles—messengers of the gospel, leaders of the church. Jesus left in part because he desired that the disciples "grow up," become mature in their faith. God desires that for us as well. Jesus said, "The person who trusts me will not only do what I'm doing but even greater things." (John 14:12, *THE MESSAGE*) God desires that we grow up in our faith. Like Michelangelo's God who lets Adam loose in the world, our God lets us loose as well in order that our faith will be grounded not simply in the tangible soil of our senses but in the depths of our heart and spirit.

Our prayer life and the spiritual discipline necessary to make it fruitful is a channel through which we receive the Holy Spirit, the Counselor promised by Jesus. It is a means by which that "so close but yet so far" feeling is lessened. It is an avenue through which, in the words of Thomas Merton, we "renew the kind of life in which the closeness [of God] is felt and experienced." (Quoted by Brennan Manning, *The Ragamuffin Gospel*, Multnomah, 1990, 2000; page 46)

Yet the tempo of the daily activity of our lives seems to impinge on that closeness. Brennan Manning tells a story that helps us at this point. A stressed business executive searched out a desert father complaining about his frustration with prayer, his flawed virtue, and his failed relationships. The hermit listened carefully and then disappeared into the darkness of his cave returning with a basin and pitcher of water.

"Watch the water as I pour it into the basin," he instructed the businessman. The water splashed against the bottom and sides of the basin, swirling and agitated. As the man watched, the water churned and eddied but gradually began to settle, the small fast ripples changing into larger swells that gently rocked back and forth, slowing until finally the surface became so smooth he could see his reflection. "That is the way it is when you live constantly in the midst of others," said the old man. "You do not see yourself as you really are because of all the confusion and disturbance. You fail to recognize the divine presence in your life, and the consciousness of your belovedness slowly fades." (Brennan Manning, *Reflections for Ragamuffins*, HarperCollinsPublishers, 1998; page 38) Just as it takes time for water to settle, so it takes time for us to connect with God, to feel God's closeness, to come to interior stillness. Without deliberate effort, without taking the time necessary to focus on God and God's place in the activities of daily living, we risk stirring up the waters of our lives and thus increasing the distance between God's fingers and ours.

Reflecting and Recording

How is the pace of your life stirring up the waters of your soul and impinging on your closeness with God?

How might you "renew the kind of life in which the closeness [of God] is felt and experienced"? What would you have to eliminate? What would you have to add?

During the Day

Take whatever steps are necessary to begin moving toward a life in which the closeness of God is felt and experienced.

DAY THREE: HARNESSED

I lift my eyes to you,
O God, enthroned in heaven.
We look to the Lord our God for his mercy,
just as servants keep their eyes on their master,
as a slave girl watches her mistress for the slightest signal.
(*Psalm 123:1-2,* New Living Translation*)*

Like many in my generation, I have always had a bit of a problem with authority. My nature is to question (at least in my own mind) persons and institutions of authority before I deliberately place myself under their direction. This posture of questioning never seemed problematic until I realized that it carried over to my relationship with God. Our relationship with God is in part about our posture. What kind of posture we assume in our relationship with God will have a great deal of impact on our ability to know God more deeply and to make God the main thing in our lives.

Psalm 123, which opens our reading today, describes the posture we must assume if we are to meaningfully experience God as the main thing in our lives. It is a psalm of ascent—a song people sang as they went up the hill to worship in the Temple in Jerusalem. It describes a posture of looking up—I lift my eyes to you. That is the posture we assume in our spiritual journey; we look up.

The problem with this posture is that it does not come naturally for us. Our more natural posture is a horizontal one. We want to explore our spirituality but on our own independent terms. Deepak Chopra is a popular secular spiritual guru who said, "I satisfy a spiritual yearning without making people think they have to worry about God or punishment." (Quoted by Mike Slaughter in "Blessed Are the Harnessed," sermon preached at Ginghamsburg Church, October 25–26, 1997) We want to be spiritual, but we do not want that spirituality to be encumbered by authority. We want to discover divinity within us or around us, but not above us. We want a God on our own level; a God we can argue with about the things that make us uncomfortable—marriage, divorce, sexuality, what we do with our money. We're not looking up; we're looking across.

Psalm 123 describes a posture of looking up. I lift my eyes to you, O God, enthroned in heaven. It is easy to avoid the issue of authority and get sidetracked by physical location when we read this psalm; but my relationship with God is not about where God is located, in the heavens or anywhere else. My relationship with God is about God's position of authority in my life.

Verse two emphasizes God's authority as well; we look to God in the same way that servants look to their masters, waiting for the slightest signal to direct them into action. That type of attitude is difficult for us because our culture stresses independence. We grow up anticipating one day leaving home; we go to school anticipating graduation and a new job. Each milestone in life marks another step on our road toward independence. What we don't realize is that independence does not always mean freedom. We are all harnessed in one way or another. As we negotiate each milestone of our life, we simply trade one harness for another. We may be excited about living on our own until we realize that now we have to pay for everything. I remember being so excited to stay home with my children—no more constraints of work; I would not have to answer to anyone. Ha! Anyone with children knows that I simply removed myself from the harness of employment in order to put on the harness of parenthood!

The wide and varying commitments of our lives harness us whether willingly or unwillingly. School, jobs, mortgages, children, parents, volunteer responsibilities, these and countless others, all come with a yoke that we must wear. That is why Jesus' words in Matthew are so important. "Take my yoke upon you. Let me teach you, because I am humble and gentle, and you will find rest for your souls. For my yoke fits perfectly, and the burden I give you is light." (Matthew 11:29-30, New Living Translation) Jesus says, "my yoke" because he knows we are already harnessed; but he wants us to be yoked in a way that is suited to us. Life will harness you; but you can choose to what or to whom you will be yoked.

Jesus says, fasten yourself to my harness, yoke yourself on God's terms, not those of the world.

There is a mythical story about a sea captain who was guiding his ship on a very dark night and saw faint lights in the distance. He told his signalman to send a message. "Alter your course 10 degrees south." A prompt message returned, "Alter your course 10 degrees north." The captain became angry because his command had been ignored, so he sent a second message, "Alter your course 10 degrees south—I am the Captain!" Again, a message promptly returned, "Alter your course 10 degrees north—I am Seaman Third Class Jones." Infuriated, the captain sent off a third message, knowing that it would evoke fear, "Alter your course 10 degrees south—I am a battleship!" Once again a prompt reply came, "Alter your course 10 degrees north—I am a lighthouse."

When we look straight ahead, often all we can see is darkness and fog. We are unable to see the forces that have us harnessed and are telling us which direction we should go, how we should behave, what commitments we should or should not make. But when we look up, when we lift our eyes as the psalmist says, we can see the light. When we yoke ourselves to Christ, recognize his authority in our lives, we become connected to God's hand and are able to follow God's light. It is God's power and energy that pulls us and pushes us and leads us.

We are focusing on prayer and its importance as we seek to know God and make God the main thing in our lives. As we commit ourselves to the discipline required to deepen our connection to God through prayer, we must do so with a posture of looking up. God is not merely a cosmic waiter, standing ready to jump at our beck and call. Our God is enthroned in the heavens and only when we look up will we be able to see God's light and be guided by it as we negotiate the activity of our daily lives.

Reflecting and Recording

Where do you "look" when you want to see God? Up? Across? Why do you want to find God there?

To what are you harnessed?

What would you have to change in order to be more fully harnessed to Christ?

During the Day

Do one thing today that will move you closer to taking off the yoke of the world and putting on more fully the yoke of Christ.

DAY FOUR: THE ANSWERING PLACE

The LORD is righteous in everything he does;
he is filled with kindness.
The LORD is close to all who call on him,
yes, to all who call on him sincerely.
He fulfills the desires of those who fear him;
he hears their cries for help and rescues them.
The LORD protects all those who love him,
but he destroys the wicked.
(Psalm 145:17-20, New Living Translation*)*

In *Jesus in Blue Jeans: A Practical Guide to Everyday Spirituality,* Laurie Beth Jones tells of serving as the executive director of a YWCA Girl's camp. There was a girl, Carol, at the camp who had been a tremendous challenge to her. One day Carol invited Laurie Beth to walk with her up the mountain. About two-thirds of the way up, Carol stepped off the trail and asked Laurie Beth to look down. When she did, she saw a small area a few yards off the path, which had been cleared of all the weeds and brush and was surrounded by a carefully constructed circle of rocks. "I cleared away everything but the wildflowers," Carol said self-consciously as Laurie Beth looked around. "From here you can see all of us down below," she said as she pointed out the recreation field and each of the cabins. "That is why I picked this spot." Carol continued tentatively, "I know I've been a lot of trouble for you . . . and I thought this might be a good place for you to come and get some answers." Laurie Beth responded, "That is beautiful, Carol. I will call this 'The Answering Place.' " (Laurie Beth Jones,

Jesus in Blue Jeans: A Practical Guide to Everyday Spirituality, Hyperion, 1997; page 151–52)

On Day One and Day Two of this week, we talked about the connections and closeness between God and us that are enhanced and strengthened through spiritual discipline and prayer. That connection and closeness is crucial if we are to meaningfully connect our faith to the activity of our daily lives. The very act of living confronts us with questions at every turn—questions about how we should behave, what we should believe, questions about our commitments, our priorities, our decision-making. Yet, many of us go through our lives without realizing that there is a place where we can go for answers. Like the water poured into the hermit's bowl, the turbulence of our lives blocks us from seeing that God is close by and available, ready to meet us wherever we are in order to hear us and respond.

Moses often went up the mountain to the place where he would meet God and receive direction. When Elijah was fleeing from Jezebel's soldiers, he went into the wilderness, encountered God in a still small voice, and discovered what he was to do next. As the time for Jesus' crucifixion drew near, he went to the Mount of Olives to pray. It was his "answering place." He knew God would be there to meet him, to listen, to answer all the questions he may have had and to guide him into his future.

As we work to integrate our faith with our daily lives, we need to be deliberate about creating answering places where we can meet God. Too often we act in haste, obtaining information but never taking enough time to carefully contemplate what we have learned. We are faced with decisions and challenges but work to address them without tapping any of our faith resources. We need to step away, find a place and time where we can meet God, open ourselves to God's movement within us, and seek God's guidance and creative power in our lives. Laurie Beth Jones writes, "I need a viewpoint that allows me to look down on the everyday happenings of my life and see them as God sees them, placed in their proper perspective." (page 152) That is a viewpoint we all need; that is a viewpoint that strengthens the connection between faith and daily life. But we will be unable to gain such a viewpoint without deliberately seeking answering places, places where we can go to meet God, to come to know God better, and that allow God to innervate the center of our lives.

Reflecting and Recording

Do you have an answering place? If so, where is it and how often do you go there?

How might your viewpoint change if you were to begin to meet God regularly in an answering place? How might that affect your decision-making?

During the Day

As you are faced with decisions today, practice being still, even if it is for a brief moment. Go in your mind to your answering place and listen for God's voice.

DAY FIVE: TRUSTING OUR INSTINCTS

When Jesus came to the region of Caesarea Philippi, he asked his disciples,
"Who do people say that the Son of Man is?"
"Well," they replied, "some say John the Baptist, some say Elijah,
and others say Jeremiah or one of the other prophets."
Then he asked them, "Who do you say I am?"
Simon Peter answered, "You are the Messiah, the Son of the living God."
Jesus replied, "You are blessed, Simon son of John, because my Father in heaven
has revealed this to you. You did not learn this from any human being.
Now I say to you that you are Peter, and upon this rock I will build my church,
and all the powers of hell will not conquer it.
(Matthew 16:13-18, New Living Translation*)*

At five, my nephew, Jacob, is very in tune with his instincts. Frequently when playing with his friends, if things start to get out of hand in some way or move in a risky direction, he can be heard to say cautiously, "I don't know, I've got a bad feeling about this. . . . " Throughout Scripture we see stories of persons who were able to trust their instincts as they followed God. They were aware of the ways and dangers of the world; and as they lived out their faith, they trusted their instincts not only as a source of protection but as a signal of how to follow God. Much to the displeasure of his opponents, Nehemiah dedicated himself to rebuilding the wall. His enemies, Sanballat and Tobiah, made several attempts to get him to stop; but at each turn he recognized that "they were just trying to intimidate us, imagining that they could break our resolve and stop the work. So I prayed for strength to continue the work." (Nehemiah 6:9, New Living

Translation) Finally, under the guise of trying to keep him safe, a friend urged him to stop working and go to the safety of the Temple; but Nehemiah's instinct told him "that God had not spoken to him, but that he had uttered this prophecy against me because Tobiah and Sanballat had hired him." (Nehemiah 6:12, New Living Translation)

Jesus had an innate sense of who was trustworthy and who was not. When the Pharisees were questioning in their hearts Jesus' pronouncements of forgiveness, believing them to be blasphemous, Jesus "perceived in his spirit" their thoughts and confronted them (Mark 2:8, New Revised Standard Version). When Peter declared him to be the Messiah, Jesus pronounced him the rock on which he would build the church, a profound sign of his trust that Peter would come through for him in the end.

Our inner instincts are a significant source of guidance as our lives unfold. While there remains much to learn about how instinct operates, I believe it is the prompting of God's Holy Spirit within us. William Law was an 18th-century English clergyman whose writings have been very influential. He described this prompting well when he wrote:

> *The book of all books is in your own heart, in which are written and engraven*
> *the deepest lessons of divine instruction; learn therefore to be deeply attentive*
> *to the presence of God in your hearts, who is always speaking, always instructing,*
> *always illuminating that heart that is attentive to him.*
> (Joy of the Saints, *Templegate, 1988; page 90*)

Our instincts are the natural means in which God communicates with us about truths we have no other way of comprehending. Learning to trust those instincts, being deeply attentive to the presence of God in our hearts, enables us to more thoroughly integrate our faith into our daily lives. It is a means through which we become more in tune with our instincts, more attentive to the inner voice of God communicating with us. Prayer, along with other spiritual disciplines, is the way in which we learn to trust the inner promptings we receive as we negotiate the challenges of life.

I find it interesting that our intestines are lined with the same type of tissue that surrounds our brains. In a strange way for me that similarity seems to account for the way our "gut" communicates with us. We must be open to that communication. We must be attentive so that we can hear God speaking to us, instructing us, and illuminating us as we make the connections between our faith and the activity of our lives. In this way we will better hear when God guides us saying, "This is the way; walk in it." (Isaiah 30:21, New Revised Standard Version)

Reflecting and Recording

Reflect on your ability to trust your instincts. Describe a time when this trust proved to be an important asset.

✳

List some situations in your life when trusting your instincts led you in the right direction.

During the Day

Be in tune with what your instincts are telling you. Remember that God communicates with us through our "gut," revealing truths we have no other way of knowing.

DAY SIX: PRAYING FROM THE HEART

And so they reached Jericho. Later, as Jesus and his disciples left town, a great
crowd was following. A blind beggar named Bartimaeus (son of Timaeus)
was sitting beside the road as Jesus was going by. When Bartimaeus heard
that Jesus from Nazareth was nearby, he began to shout out,
"Jesus, Son of David, have mercy on me!"
"Be quiet!" some of the people yelled at him.
But he only shouted louder, "Son of David, have mercy on me!"
When Jesus heard him, he stopped and said, "Tell him to come here."
So they called the blind man. "Cheer up," they said. "Come on, he's calling you!"
Bartimaeus threw aside his coat, jumped up, and came to Jesus.
"What do you want me to do for you?" Jesus asked.
"Teacher," the blind man said, "I want to see!"
And Jesus said to him, "Go your way. Your faith has healed you."
And instantly the blind man could see! Then he followed Jesus down the road.
(Mark 10:46-52, New Living Translation*)*

Prayer is a powerful and productive force in our lives. It allows us to join with
God in working not only in our own lives but also in the lives of others. The
reverse is true as well. Prayer invites God to join with us in the unfolding of our
lives and the lives of those around us. Unfortunately, we often overlook prayer
as a connection to God and thus a source of direction and strength and operate
as though we were on our own.

On Day Three I mentioned that God is not some cosmic waiter standing
ready to jump at our beck and call. That is indeed true; our relationship is not

one where we stand with power and look either across or down at God, making demands at every turn of our whim or fancy. Yet, as we appropriately lift our eyes to God, God does wait with loving anticipation for us to pour out to him our deepest desires and dreams; and even more, God longs to respond to those desires and dreams as well.

In *The Life of Christian Devotion*, William Law wrote,

All outward power that we exercise in the things about us is but as a shadow in comparison of that inward power that resides in our will, imagination, and desires. . . . Our desire is not only thus powerful and productive of real effects, but it is always alive, always working and creating in us. . . . And here lies the ground of the great efficacy of prayer, which when it is the prayer of the heart, the prayer of faith, has a kindling and creating power, and forms and transforms the soul into every thing that its desires reach after. . . . It opens, extends, and moves that in us which has its being and motion in and with the divine nature, and so brings us into real union and communion with God.
(William Law, The Life of Christian Devotion, *Abingdon; pages 85–86)*

While Law's language can be difficult, his message is simple—when we are connected to God through prayer, our wills, our imaginations, our desires can have powerful results. Prayer is a creating power that, when in communion with God, forms and transforms us. God desires to answer the prayers of our hearts.

The world would have us believe that we are left to our own devices, with little power beyond ourselves. Society encourages us to look within ourselves, or to popular culture, for answers to life's difficult questions, for insight into managing the competing demands and commitments of daily life, and for aid in determining how our faith fits the larger picture of our lives, when the ultimate power to face all those issues is right before us, quietly waiting to be invited into the discussion.

When Jesus encountered individuals in his ministry, frequently he asked them, "What do you want?" Only when they responded with the prayer of their heart—"Teacher, I want to see!"—did he act on their desire. Jesus assured us that God knows our needs before we even ask; yet, that knowing never preempts the asking process. If we long to know God, if we truly desire to make God the main thing in our lives, we must be willing to tell God exactly that. Only then will we encounter the kindling and creating power of prayer that will not only draw us into communion with God but will also open us to God's transforming energy in our lives.

Reflecting and Recording

What is the prayer of your heart today?

Spend some quiet time in making that prayer known to God.

✳

During the Day

As you move through the day, remember that when we are connected to God through prayer, our wills, our imaginations, and our desires can have powerful results. Channel that power.

DAY SEVEN: CREATING THE YET TO BE

You can ask for anything in my name, and I will do it, because the work of the Son brings glory to the Father. Yes, ask anything in my name, and I will do it! (*John 14:13-14,* New Living Translation)

Yesterday we talked about God's yearning not only to hear about our deepest desires and dreams but also to respond to those desires and dreams as well. That is at the heart of this great promise from Jesus, "Ask anything in my name, and I will do it!" Yet so often we limit this promise to the realm of getting things—asking for God to meet our basic needs or desires. We live as though we are unaware of the productive and creating power of prayer that Laurie Beth Jones described as "the shaping power of the future." (Laurie Beth Jones, *Jesus in Blue Jeans: A Practical Guide to Everyday Spirituality,* Hyperion, 1997; page 122)

Prayer is the force God places at our disposal in order that we might create what is yet to be. While I am not gifted in the area of science, physics has often fascinated me, particularly when I engage in conversations with those who study it at a high level. Where I stand speechless in the face of the mystery of the universe, they seem to be able to describe it and the way it works with great ease and eloquence. One area of study that I find intriguing is that of quantum mechanics, the study of subatomic interactions. Researchers in this field theorize and offer evidence that the world does not come into being until a mind interacts with it. They have conducted experiments in which measuring the spin of one subatomic particle has, oddly enough, caused a twin particle miles away to have the opposite spin! It is as though the observer is *creating* reality.

An equally mind-boggling finding has come from research in quantum physics where particles have been discovered that take on properties in direct proportion to the *expectations* of the people watching them. While I cannot comprehend the full meaning of that discovery, it brings to my mind the image of millions of creative particles floating in our universe, each awaiting our direct instruction.

David Miller's book, *The Lord of Bellavista*, recounts the dramatic transformation that took place during the 1990s in Colombia's Bellavista National Jail, one of the most dangerous prisons in the world. Central to that transformation was the work of Oscar Osorio, a drug-addicted, violent criminal in Villa Hermosa, Colombia. Oscar had grown up poor, resorting to stealing when he was still a young boy. He graduated to drug dealing, armed robbery, and violence. By the time he was in his late twenties, he had been in and out of jail numerous times, including Bellavista. One day in 1983, as he was sleeping off a drug binge that had left him lying on a sheet of cardboard for three days in a semiconscious stupor, he encountered pastor Jairo Chalarca who, as he passed, looked at Oscar and said, "Jesus loves you and he wants to change your life." Somehow those words penetrated Oscar's drug-clouded head, and he looked up with interest. Chalarca began talking with him about the plans God had for him, plans far greater than sleeping on cardboard on the street, plans that had yet to be. He invited Oscar to church. Surprisingly, Oscar got up and followed him. He does not remember the details of Pastor Chalarca's sermon that day, nor does he remember what Scriptures were read; but as he listened to Pastor Chalarca preach that day, Oscar wept for the first time in years. He felt himself begin to change. He heard Chalarca say, "Jesus Christ knows you. He knows exactly what condition you are in. If you come to know Christ, he will raise you up. He will change your life. If you want to meet Christ today, come forward to the front of the church and we will pray with you."

Oscar went to the front of the church and told Pastor Chalarca he wanted the life he was speaking of, he wanted to know Jesus. Jairo put his hands on Oscar's shoulders and began to pray. Afterwards, Oscar had difficulty putting into words what happened to him during that prayer; but he said it was something like feeling that a ton of weight was bearing down on him and he could not get out from under it. The weight was crushing him, suffocating him; but suddenly it was lifted, and he felt buoyant, strong, and free. The freedom gained from that prayer innervated his life. He stopped doing drugs; he left his life of crime and violence behind; and the plans that had yet to be began to take shape in his life. He got a job, became active in his church, and by 1987 began fulltime ministry, preaching the gospel to prisoners in Bellavista, thus sparking a transformation of the prison unlike any other. (David Miller, *The Lord of Bellavista*, Triangle, 1998; pages 30–33)

Describing the change initiated by Oscar's work, Miller writes:

> *The same prison that once claimed 50 lives a month has averaged
> only one homicide per year since 1990, when Oscar Osorio envisioned God
> wrapping the jail in his hand and received divine orders to raise white flags
> and pray. During the same six-year period, Oscar baptized 514 inmates
> in a makeshift baptistery in the prison chapel. Christian conversions
> have replaced murders as Bellavista's most impressive statistic.*
> *(David Miller,* The Lord of Bellavista, *Triangle, 1998; page 142)*

Certainly not all of us have stories as dramatic as Oscar Osorio. Yet, through his experience of Jesus Christ made manifest through prayer, he was able to see his future, not as a weight crushing down upon him, but as a blank canvas upon which he and God would write.

We are granted the opportunity to experience that as well. Our lives may be complicated and busy. It may be challenging to connect God to our everyday lives. There may be elements of our lives that hem us in, weigh us down, and stress us out. But regardless of how difficult our present may be, our future is a blank canvas placed before us. Through prayer we are given the opportunity to participate in the works of God in the world—to join with God in creating what is yet to be—to write with God upon the canvas of our lives. Like the particles that hover in our universe waiting to comply with our expectations, we join with God in creating what is yet to be through the creative power of prayer.

Reflecting and Recording

Jesus promised that if we ask for anything in his name, he will respond. What do you want your "yet to be" to look like? Make a few notes to get that "yet to be" firmly in your mind. Enter into a time of prayer as you bring this dream before God.

Conclude your time of prayer by asking God to keep you aware of the ongoing, creative power of all your thoughts and words.

During the Day

As you move through the day, be aware of the tools you might use as you partner with God in creating the yet to be.

GROUP MEETING FOR WEEK THREE

Introduction

Christian fellowship requires two essential elements, feedback and follow-up. The group dynamic will not work positively for everyone without feedback; and follow-up is vital to the expression of Christian concern and ministry. The leader is the primary person responsible for feedback in the group; however, everyone should feel free to share their feelings about how the group is functioning. Listening is crucial. It is, as much as any other action, a means of affirmation. Our listening sends the message that the other is important, that we value her. Equally important is the process of checking out meaning so that those who are sharing this journey with us will know that we are really hearing them. It is easy to hear incorrectly or to misinterpret what we hear. "Are you saying . . . ?" is a good way to clarify.

Everyone has a responsibility to follow up. Listening to what others are saying will make us aware of varying degrees of need and concern, of situations deserving special prayer and attention. Taking notes is important as the group shares. With the aid of these notes, you will be able to follow up during the week with a telephone call, a written note of caring and encouragement, or a visit. Christian fellowship is distinguished by caring translated into action, so it is essential to follow up each week with others in the group.

Sharing Together

You have now had several weeks of sharing, thus a significant amount of "knowing" probably exists within your group. Hopefully, persons are feeling safe in your group and are more willing to share. At the same time, we do not want to pressure anyone to share if they are not yet comfortable. Be particularly sensitive to any woman who is slow to share. She may need gentle coaxing and encouragement in order to feel at ease. Every person brings something special to the group. Others are able to fully experience that uniqueness through sharing.

- Reflect on the basic human yearning for something beyond ourselves—the desire to be connected to something, even though we may not be sure what that something is. How have you experienced that yearning? How was it connected to your decision to participate in this study?
- Think about how you might "renew the kind of life in which the closeness [of God] is felt and experienced." (See Reflecting and Recording, Day Two, page 76.) How might the group support you in this process?
- Consider your experience of being harnessed in one way or another. What steps are you taking to become more fully yoked to Christ? (See Reflecting and Recording, Day Three, page 80.) Again, how might the group support you?
- Reflect on your "yet to be" and the experience of bringing that dream before God. What tools have you discovered that might help you partner with God in creating this yet to be? What tools might the group provide?

Praying Together

One of the great blessings of the Christian community is that of praying together. You have been together now for three weeks; be a bit bolder now and experiment with the deeper blessings of group prayer by sharing more openly and intimately. Consider sharing a need in your life. These needs might include, but certainly would not be limited to

- a need to trust Christ more—to become more fully yoked to him;
- the pain of living out the consequences of something you have done in the past;
- an unwillingness to forgive someone who has done something for which you are suffering;
- a failure to invest yourself in love because you think the situation is hopeless.

As you join together in prayer, feel free to offer verbal prayers for those who have shared specific needs and/or concerns. You might find meaning in closing your time together by singing a chorus or a verse of a hymn or praise song that everyone knows, such as "Amazing Grace," "Jesus Loves Me," or "I Love You, Lord" and/or by praying together the Lord's Prayer.

Week Four:
A Life of Moral Excellence

DAY ONE: USEFUL KNOWLEDGE

As we know Jesus better, his divine power gives us everything we need for living a godly life. He has called us to receive his own glory and goodness! And by that same mighty power, he has given us all of his rich and wonderful promises. He has promised that you will escape the decadence all around you caused by evil desires and that you will share in his divine nature. So make every effort to apply the benefits of these promises to your life. Then your faith will produce a life of moral excellence. A life of moral excellence leads to knowing God better. Knowing God leads to self-control. Self-control leads to patient endurance, and patient endurance leads to godliness. Godliness leads to love for other Christians, and finally you will grow to have genuine love for everyone. The more you grow like this, the more you will become productive and useful in your knowledge of our Lord Jesus Christ.
(2 Peter 1:3-8, New Living Translation*)*

We are now midway through this six-week adventure. We have been exploring how Scripture can become more relevant to our daily lives—how we can come to know God better and place God more firmly at the center of our lives. To this end, we have discussed our convictions regarding Scripture, searched our faith to discover where we are on our journey, and delved into the spiritual discipline of prayer. By now you may be asking, "When will she tell me what I can actually *do*?" While this is not a "how to" manual by any means, I believe it is possible for us to live out our faith in visible, tangible ways—there are things we can "do" that indicate to the world that God is at the center of our lives and that we take the witness of Scripture seriously in the choices we make and the commitments we undertake. These things that we "do" are the activities and actions that make up our moral life—the godly life as Peter refers to it.

Our behavior and our faith are intimately intertwined as is reflected in the Scripture we read today. Peter writes, "As we know Jesus better, his divine power gives us everything we need for living a godly life." Clearly deepening our relationship with Christ is crucial if we are to live lives of moral significance. Conversely, living a "life of moral excellence leads to knowing God better." There is an obvious interdependency here. Rather than being a neatly packaged set of "steps" that if followed to the letter will instantly make us morally excellent or magically place God at the center of our lives, our faith experience is a process of deepening our relationship with God through prayer and spiritual discipline, through the study of Scripture, and through a commitment to the moral life. Each of these components in turn strengthens the others as the process continues for the entirety of our lives. As our faith grows, our knowledge about Christ, about Scripture, about the various tenets of the Christian faith becomes productive and useful; that experience then deepens our faith, and on it goes.

How then do we begin to be "more productive and useful in our knowledge of Jesus Christ"? How do we strengthen our moral lives? The foundation for such an undertaking is very simple—we begin with moral sincerity. We must truly *want* to live a moral life; we must earnestly desire to apply Scripture to our daily lives with integrity and power. There may be some of us who need to start one step earlier. We may need to begin by asking God to *help us* want to live a moral life. A deliberate commitment to moral integrity that extends beyond simply wanting to "be a good person" may be something that has been externally placed upon us rather than springing from within ourselves. Thus, our first task is to ask God to help us desire that deeper commitment, to help us actually *want* it rather than feeling we ought to have it.

Beginning with moral sincerity is closely connected to the faith issues raised in Week Two. As we begin the process of strengthening our moral selves, we must start where we are. We must ask for and accept the forgiveness God offers in order to be free from the guilt of the past that so often constrains us. For some of us this is an ongoing part of our spiritual journey, but for others this may be a giant first step. Regardless of where you are on your journey, moral sincerity is a gift from God; for it is God whose divine power gives us everything we need to live a godly life.

A second foundation for a commitment to the moral life is the community of faith. Moral excellence is a "lived reality" that is strengthened by the community of believers. As social beings, we are constantly being shaped by the culture that surrounds us. Thus, if we are to succeed in our commitment to the moral life, we must surround ourselves with others who treasure virtue, who are dedicated to teaching and living the moral life. This study may be helpful on a personal level. It may launch you on your journey toward knowing God more deeply and living in ways that reflect that relationship. However, our striving to apply Scripture to our daily lives with integrity and power—to live out our faith in visible and tangible ways, to make God the main thing in our lives—that striving will not be consistently rewarding without the support of a morally serious community committed to providing direction and encouragement.

Knowing God and making God the main thing does involve action. We commit ourselves to Scripture, to prayer, and to living in ways that reflect our faith. In other words, we *behave* in ways that reflect God's place at the center of our lives. This behavior is not confined to specific activities such as church attendance; but it extends to our daily lives and all the decisions and actions that take place there. This week will focus on the doing—the behavior involved in knowing God and making God the main thing in our lives. A final word from *The Workbook on Virtues and the Fruit of the Spirit* is appropriate at this point:

Simplicity and a sense of humor are always assets to any spiritual endeavor. If you know something is wrong, simply don't do it; and in all things remember that virtue is much too serious an endeavor to be solemn. An ability to laugh at our mistakes and foibles will lighten our load as we journey through the moral life. (Maxie Dunnam and Kimberly Dunnam Reisman, The Workbook on Virtues and the Fruit of the Spirit, *1998; page 28)*

Reflecting and Recording

In what ways do you genuinely want to strengthen the moral fabric of your life?

Are you connected to persons who are committed to the moral life? If so, how has that connection benefited you as you seek to connect your faith to your daily life? If not, how might you develop a relationship with such a community? How might the group aid you in this endeavor?

Make a list of people who have mentored you in the process of applying Scripture to your daily life with integrity and power. What is it about them that drew you to them? Describe those characteristics and interactions.

During the Day

Take a simple step toward living in ways that reflect God's place at the center of your life by using this guide for your life today: *If something is wrong, simply don't do it.*

DAY TWO: EMPOWERING GRACE

And God is able to make all grace abound to you, so that in all things at all times,
having all that you need, you will abound in every good work.
(2 Corinthians 9:8, New International Version)

Yesterday we discussed the fact that commitment to moral integrity is crucial to knowing God and making God the main thing in our lives. The experience of faith is not a one-time, all-at-once experience; rather it is a process—a journey. Because it is a journey, we grow as various components of our faith strengthen each other. As we read yesterday in Peter, in knowing Jesus better, his divine power gives us everything we need to live a godly life. Our faith then produces a life of moral excellence. A life of moral excellence, in turn, leads to knowing God better. Thus the cycle of spiritual formation begins and continues with the result being that the more we grow, the more we become productive and useful in our knowledge of Christ.

It is important to recognize the cyclical nature of spiritual growth; however, if my understanding stops there, it is easy to believe that I, in and of myself, am responsible for my own spiritual development. Yes, it is up to us to make deliberate choices about our spiritual growth—to pay attention to that aspect of our lives (or not), to commit ourselves to discipline (or not), to actively seek God (or not). While true, that is not the entire picture. There is another aspect of spiritual formation that is crucial if we are to avoid misunderstanding spiritual growth (which includes developing our moral lives) as an endeavor of works righteousness.

Actively living out our faith through our behavior and actions is not the means through which we are reconciled with God. That activity is a *result* of being reconciled with God. Echoing Paul's words to the Corinthians that began today's reading, it is God's grace within us that enables us to abound in every good work. Recall our discussion on Day Three of Week Two. I asserted then that God's grace is the means through which our relationship with God is restored. What we call justifying grace is the redemptive, healing, recreating love of God. It is a gift that we receive not because we deserve it, or have earned it, but because God freely gives it. Justifying grace is God's radical love for us, a love that is more powerful than sin, that reconciles our relationship and "makes us right" with God.

Understanding the process of spiritual formation includes understanding that God's grace does not stop working within us simply because we have accepted it and experienced justification. It is not that our own efforts suddenly take over where God's grace leaves off. On the contrary, once we have accepted God's forgiving, reconciling, justifying grace, that same grace enters a new phase of activity in our lives. This new phase of activity is what theologians call the work of *sanctifying* grace. As we live our lives, God's sanctifying grace works within us to strengthen us and give us the power to face whatever challenges we encounter as well as to shape us into the likeness of Christ. When we seek to develop our moral lives in order to live out our faith in visible ways, we are not simply exercising our will to behave in a certain way, or undertaking certain actions; we are making ourselves available to become channels of God's grace, both for the benefit of our own spiritual growth and for the benefit of others who may be touched by that grace through us. Paul described it vividly when he wrote to the Corinthians, "Whatever I am now, it is all because God poured out his special favor on me—and not without results. . . . Yet it was not I but God who was working through me by his grace." (1 Corinthians 15:10, New Living Translation)

Sanctifying grace, then, is our source of power as we seek to make God the main thing in our lives and live in ways that reflect that to the world. It is the strength of God's love that recreates us and enables us to move toward moral excellence, which in turn fosters our relationship with God, thus energizing the cycle of spiritual growth.

Reflecting and Recording

Understanding that the Christian experience is a process fueled by sanctifying grace, write a paragraph about significant events, changes, experiences, or relationships that have played a role in your spiritual formation. It may be helpful to remind yourself of your experience with justifying grace by referring back to the Reflecting and Recording section on Day Three of Week Two (page 53).

During the Day

Sanctifying grace is most often experienced in the context of daily living. It is not an exclusive "mountain top" encounter; rather sanctifying grace is rooted in the living out of the ordinary daily activities that ground our existence, in our everyday actions and attitudes. Be aware of situations today when you need the power of sanctifying grace. Claim that power as you seek to live out your faith in real and visible ways.

DAY THREE: BEARING FRUIT

Oh, the joys of those
who do not follow the advice of the wicked,
or stand around with sinners,
or join in with scoffers.
But they delight in doing everything the LORD *wants,*
day and night they think about his law.
They are like trees planted along the riverbank,
bearing fruit each season without fail.
Their leaves never wither,
and in all they do, they prosper.
(Psalm 1:1-3, New Living Translation*)*

On Day One of this week, I asserted that we can do things that indicate to the world that God is at the center of our lives and that we take the witness of Scripture seriously in the choices we make and the commitments we undertake. These actions make up our moral life. For Christians, there should be little, if any, difference between our "moral" life and our everyday life. The moral values that ground the Christian faith should permeate every aspect of our lives. The Psalms liken this kind of life to trees planted along a riverbank, bearing fruit year after year. That is a wonderful metaphor for what our lives look like when God becomes the main thing.

I love to garden. I enjoy flowerbeds and containers filled with blooms. Unfortunately, my prowess with indoor plants lags greatly behind my outdoor capabilities. Thankfully I have improved substantially and can now actually keep a plant alive within my home. I have a friend, Phyllis, who, unlike me, has a wonderful green thumb, particularly when it comes to houseplants. At any given time you can enter her home and there will be violets, cactus, and other plants, beautifully healthy, many with scads of blossoms. I recall seeing a lovely Christmas cactus in full bloom in her living room. I was amazed because I had a cactus just like it, minus the blooms. I did not even realize that it *could* bloom, because mine had never had a single blossom. Ever since seeing the beauty of Phyllis's cactus, I have been disappointed in my own, which is not an unattractive plant—it is actually a lovely deep green and very healthy. But it has never truly achieved its purpose and thus every time I look at it, I feel a sense of disappointment.

We were meant to bear fruit in our spiritual lives—not just interior fruit as our faith deepens, but external fruit, fruit that shows itself in the way that we live. If we develop our faith in such a way that we are healthy and our spiritual lives are like my cactus, "not unattractive" but have never born fruit or blossoms, there will always be an underlying sense of disappointment. We will not have achieved our entire purpose. James was pointing us toward this truth when he asked, "Dear brothers and sisters, what's the use of saying you have faith if you don't prove it by your actions?" (James 2:14, New Living Translation) We are at our best when we have God's Word ever before us and in live ways that reflect that. When we "delight in doing everything the LORD wants," we too become "like trees planted along the riverbank, bearing fruit each season without fail."

Reflecting and Recording

Spend a few minutes reflecting on your own life. What kind of fruit are you bearing as you journey in your faith?

✳

Make a list of the ways in which your faith is bearing fruit. What activities or actions make your faith visible to others? How might your faith life bear more fruit? What would you have to change to become more fruitful in your spiritual life?

During the Day

As the activities of your day unfold, be particularly aware of ways in which you can put your faith into action.

DAY FOUR: HEARING AND DOING

But be doers of the word, and not merely hearers who deceive themselves. For if any are hearers of the word and not doers, they are like those who look at themselves in a mirror; for they look at themselves and, on going away, immediately forget what they were like. But those who look into the perfect law, the law of liberty, and persevere, being not hearers who forget but doers who act—they will be blessed in their doing.
(*James 1:22-25,* New Revised Standard Version*)*

While we rest our faith solidly on God's gift of grace, James rightly points out the importance of the way we conduct our lives. Merely saying we want to know God more deeply and make God the main thing in our lives will not result in that happening unless we take action to make it happen. Talking about strengthening the connections between Scripture and our daily lives will not magically produce those connections unless we work toward that end through the way we act and live. We have talked about some of the action we can take to move God to the center of our lives—prayer and spiritual discipline, undertaking an honest examination of where we are in our faith, exploring the power of Scripture in our lives, to name a few. You have been acting with the guidance of this workbook to enhance your relationship with God and move God more firmly into the center of your life. Yesterday we discussed the concept of bearing fruit as a result of our relationship with God—fruit that takes the form of action in our lives, the visible ways we live out our faith. The details of that action will vary for each of us, but there are several foundational elements that should ground the activity of our lives and be common to all of us, given our commitment to Christ and our desire to make our faith more relevant to our daily lives. Those foundational elements are often referred to as the cardinal virtues. They are *wisdom, courage, justice, temperance, faith, hope,* and *love.* For the next several days, I would like to focus on two of these virtues, justice and temperance, which I believe are crucial to living in ways that reflect the reality that God is indeed the main thing in our lives. If we are to be doers of the Word and not merely hearers, as James suggests, we must have a foundation upon which to stand as we act. Clearly Scripture is our foundation as we are to be doers of the *Word.* An outgrowth of Scripture that contributes to the strength of that foundation is the virtue of justice.

We are living in difficult times. Many associate this difficulty predominantly with terrorism and the ongoing possibility of war around the world. Certainly these are major factors in the troubles facing our country and world; yet, there is another component to our problems that is subtler, constantly brewing beneath the surface of our consciousness, only now and again bubbling, often violently, to the forefront of our awareness. That component is the crisis of justice.

In the United States we often falsely believe there is no crisis. We like to believe that justice is one of our strengths as a nation—we were founded on the principle of "liberty and justice for all" and the Civil Rights Movement ended the era of Jim Crow. But there is a crisis of justice, here and abroad. People are hurt and killed because of the color of their skin or sexual orientation. People are denied work because of their age or gender. Elderly persons are abandoned, children are neglected, and poor people are ignored. One of the unfortunate aftereffects of the World Trade Center and Pentagon tragedy is that we now live with a deep distrust of anyone different from ourselves, particularly those of Islamic background. The crisis of justice that has been with us for years has now taken on a new dimension. Isaiah understood our situation. Israel was experiencing a similar crisis of justice that prompted Isaiah to cry out:

No wonder we are in darkness when we expected light. No wonder we are walking in the gloom. No wonder we grope like blind people and stumble along. Even at brightest noontime, we fall down as though it were dark. . . . We look for justice, but it is nowhere to be found. . . . Truth falls dead in the streets, and fairness has been outlawed. Yes, truth is gone, and anyone who tries to live a godly life is soon attacked.

The Lord looked and was displeased to find that there was no justice.
He was amazed to see that no one intervened to help the oppressed.
(Isaiah 59:9-11, 14-16; New Living Translation*)*

In its classic sense, justice is simply giving each person his or her due. This understanding of justice, from which our modern conceptions are derived, begins with the individual and over time has developed a pronounced legal flavor. Biblical justice, the understanding of justice that undergirds our faith, is much more complex than that. It connects with the way we feel, how we relate to others, what we value, and the priorities we set. Justice undergirds our faith, not because it is an important virtue on which civil society depends, but because it is an attribute of God. That is why it must ground our actions as we seek to make connections between our faith and daily life, because to ignore the cry of those suffering injustice is to ignore the cry of God.

Where classical justice is individualistic and legalistic, biblical justice is relational and intimately connected to righteousness. Righteousness focuses on the power of God that sets things right and heals relationships, communities, nations, and the world:

Thus says the LORD:
"Keep justice, and do righteousness,
for My salvation is about to come,
and My righteousness to be revealed."
(Isaiah 56:1, New King James Version)

Rather than focusing as classical justice does solely on external factors such as how individuals are related to and exist within society, righteousness contains both external and internal dimensions. The external dimension, our individual relationship with society, is important; but righteousness adds the internal dimension as well, an emphasis on our relationship with God. Understanding these two dimensions of righteousness, the personal and the social, is crucial if we are to live in ways that indicate that God is the main thing in our lives.

But how do we live so that our understanding of righteousness is evident? Clearly, we begin with ourselves. The social dimension of righteousness only becomes a reality when people take personal righteousness seriously. That is why this is such a crucial foundation for our effort to make God the main thing in our lives. Personal righteousness, the power of God's righteousness working in us, benefits us greatly; but it is personal not private. When we commit ourselves to certain values, seeking to make strong connections between our faith and our daily lives, those values must emanate outward from us to the world. In that way we become doers of the word and not merely hearers. In that way the power of God's righteousness works not only in us but also through us—to heal relationships, communities, and the world.

The prophet Amos had an amazing vision where justice will "roll down like waters, and righteousness like an ever-flowing stream." (Amos 5:24, New Revised Standard Version) The virtue of justice that grounds our efforts to connect our faith in our daily lives is not meant to be a trickle but an ever-flowing stream. It is not meant to occur in short bursts at Christmas but to roll down continuously. In *The Workbook on Virtues and the Fruit of the Spirit* justice is described:

The rolling waters of justice depend on our personal commitment to righteousness. We are to be the ever-flowing stream, through our living out of the Ten Commandments, through our commitment to treating others as we would want them to treat us, through our loving of neighbors as we love ourselves. When we become the ever-flowing stream, rather than trickling in fits and starts, the marks of God's righteousness will be seen in our world: justice that is blind to color or gender, protection for the weak, fairness in the courts, the opportunity for honest work for all who are willing, greater care of the earth. (Maxie Dunnam and Kimberly Dunnam Reisman, The Workbook on Virtues and the Fruit of the Spirit, *Upper Room Books, 1998; page 64)*

Personal righteousness is at the heart of Amos's vision of justice. It is at the heart of our quest to make connections between our faith and our daily lives. It is at the heart of our journey toward knowing God better. Proverbs 21:3 says, "The LORD is more pleased when we do what is just and right than when we give him sacrifices." (New Living Translation) That is a telling use of words. In secular society we often speak of "getting justice," whereas the Bible talks about "doing justice." We "do justice" when we work to set things right or maintain what is already right. That type of activity involves both our personal and our communal lives. Such activity forges visible connections between our faith and our daily lives, and it provides outward and observable evidence that for us God is, in fact, the main thing.

Reflecting and Recording

Spend a few minutes thinking about the classical definition of *justice* as "giving each person his or her due."

✳

Do you know of a person or group who is not getting his, her, or their due? Describe what is going on in that situation. What are the justice issues?

Now spend a few minutes thinking about your personal feelings about justice. Are you more interested in *getting* justice or *doing* justice?

✳

What has been your experience in doing justice? Describe your efforts.

During the Day

Watch for opportunities to do justice. Take advantage of those opportunities to act.

DAY FIVE: CHRIST AT THE CENTER

Clothe yourselves with the armor of right living, as those who live in the light. . . .
Let the Lord Jesus Christ take control of you.
(Romans 13:12, 14; New Living Translation*)*

A second virtue that I believe is helpful to explore as we seek to connect our faith to our daily lives is that of temperance.

Just as biblical justice expands and deepens the classical notion, so it is with the temperance of Scripture. It expands and deepens classical temperance, which the Greeks understood as "nothing overmuch." While this virtue has gotten a bad rap over the years, it is simply the proper ordering of what is good within our natures. Rather than attempting to eliminate our natural inclinations, temperance seeks to order them, thus producing a well-ordered soul, a well-balanced self, and a well-proportioned life.

Plato viewed temperance as the rational ordering of the soul that kept it free. The opposite of temperance then is intemperance or imbalance in which the soul is not free but in bondage to a particular aspect of its nature. This bondage can occur in two ways. Part of the self can rule the whole as is evident in addictive circumstances; or the whole self can become fragmented, pulled apart by the excess of many things.

Temperance is of significant value to us as we seek to make connections between our faith and daily lives. We are confronted on an almost-daily basis with choices about how we will live our lives and the role faith will play in them. From the everyday decision whether or not to take on another volunteer responsibility at our children's school or in our community to the more weighty decisions about how much time we will commit to our jobs and/or our families, temperance is a badly needed foundation that can guide us in decision-making. Temperance protects us from being dominated by only one part of our whole selves. It keeps the drive to succeed in our careers in check and thus avoids excessive conflicts at home. It guards us from believing we need to be everything for our families in order to find personal fulfillment. Temperance protects us from the excess of many things by enabling us to avoid filling our lives with too many competing demands that can lead to a loss of balance because we no longer are able to find our center.

The temperate woman knows herself. She comprehends what is important and is able to set priorities and goals. When we are temperate, we understand the idea of delayed gratification and are willing to make sacrifices for what we want. The temperate woman tends to make wise judgments about what to do and not to do as she seeks to order her soul.

Biblical temperance is about finding balance within ourselves, but more importantly it is about being centered—centered on Christ. Again there is a deepening of the classical notion. It is not enough that the soul is well-ordered; it is to be well-ordered toward love, the love of God and the love of our neighbor. The well-ordered soul that results from temperance is not for our own benefit, although we certainly do gain from it; it is for the sake of God and neighbor. *The Workbook on Virtues and the Fruit of the Spirit* explains it this way:

In classical Greek thinking, the mind conquers all problems; thus, the root of evil is ignorance. Reason is what saves us; therefore, temperance is the rational ordering that comes through an exercise of the mind. Christian temperance is, on the surface, quite similar; but it has a completely different foundation. The biblical notion of temperance asserts that it is not ignorance but sin, that distortion of our heart, that is the root of evil. Reason alone is unable to save us. Reason can fix ignorance, but it cannot fix sin. Only Christ can fix sin. Therefore, it is not reason that produces temperance, but the Holy Spirit that indwells us when we come into relationship with Jesus Christ. Temperance, then, is the living of a Spirit-filled, Christ-centered life.
(Maxie Dunnam and Kimberly Dunnam Reisman, The Workbook on Virtues and the Fruit of the Spirit, *Upper Room Books, 1998; page 71)*

Herein lies the crux of the connection between our faith and our daily lives. As Christians, we claim Christ as the center of our lives. He is the one to whom we look to provide order for our souls, for "when Christ is the Lord of our lives, nothing else can be; when Christ is not the Lord of our lives, anything and everything else will be." *(The Workbook on Virtues and the Fruit of the Spirit,* page 71) When Christ is at the center of our lives, we are able to live temperately, with balance and order within our souls. We are able to organize our lives toward the love of God and neighbor, making decisions that are right for us and connecting our faith in visible and tangible ways to our everyday activities.

Reflecting and Recording

Reflect on the Greek notion of "nothing overmuch." How is that principle currently being reflected in your life?

$$*$$

Examine your life from the perspective of intemperance as part of the self-ruling of the entire self. Describe the ways in which one part of your self is ruling your life.

Think about the ways in which the other type of intemperance, fragmentation, or the excess of many things that pull us apart may be affecting your life. Describe two or three drives, habits, or personality traits that tend to fragment your life.

In question two you listed a part of yourself that may be ruling your entire self. How do you seek to control that part of yourself? Reflect on the ways that placing Christ at the center of your life might protect you from this type of domination.

✳

In relation to this one controlling aspect of your life, what do you need to do to be more Christ-centered and Spirit-filled?

In question three you listed several drives, habits, or personality traits that tend to fragment your life. How might these be brought into harmony by a deepened commitment to Christ at the center? How might the Spirit prevail where your own will has fallen short?

I asserted that when Christ is Lord of your life, nothing else can be; when Christ is not Lord of your life, anything and everything else will be. This statement is printed in the back of the workbook. Clip this and place it somewhere where you will be reminded of its importance. Close your time today with this prayer: Lord, enable me to live by the Spirit, keeping in step with the Spirit at each turn of my day.

During the Day

As your day unfolds, be aware of any inclination toward intemperance. Is there an area of your life that is dominating and blocking you from experiencing balance? Do you need to say "no" more often?

DAY SIX: THE PEACE OF CHRIST

*Don't worry about anything; instead, pray about everything. Tell God what you
need, and thank him for all he has done. If you do this, you will experience God's
peace, which is far more wonderful than the human mind can understand.
His peace will guard your hearts and minds as you live in Christ Jesus.
(Philippians 4:6-7,* New Living Translation*)*

On Day Three we talked about bearing fruit in our spiritual lives. We return
to that image today in a discussion of peace. Exploring the fruit of peace dif-
fers from our previous discussion in that it is not necessarily a fruit that
becomes evident because of our *activity*. Rather, it is a fruit that becomes
apparent in us through our attitude or disposition. I add it here because others can witness a strong connection between our faith and our daily lives not
only through our actions but through the very way we carry ourselves. When
we have a strong connection between our faith and our daily lives, our lives will
be marked by an inner sense of peace. This peace is not the same as a life without problems. Like the joy we discussed in Week Two, the inner peace I am
speaking of depends not on our outer circumstances; it hinges on an awareness
of the reality of our salvation and the confidence that God will meet
our needs.

The disciples are excellent examples of the inner nature of peace. As their
experience with Jesus unfolded, through his ministry, his death, and his resurrection, the disciples were never exempted from difficulties in life. Their peace
was not an external experience. On the contrary, they endured prison, interro-
gations, beatings, and were even martyred as a result of their faith. Thus the

peace that marks a life of faith is an interior one, the gift Jesus promised his disciples when he said, "I am leaving you with a gift—peace of mind and heart. And the peace I give isn't like the peace the world gives. So don't be troubled or afraid." (John 14:27, New Living Translation)

The problem for Christians is that there is a huge gap between what we profess and how we live. Similar to keeping our joy secret and hidden, we do not live as people with an internal sense of peace. We may claim to have abundant life, but the way we live does not provide much evidence that this life is superior. We may insist that we are confident that God will provide for us, but the reality of our panic at the first sign of trouble belies that assertion. It is one thing to talk about peace; it is quite another to claim it in the face of tragedy. That is why peace is such an important fruit to foster as we seek to know God and make God the main thing in our lives. The gap between what we profess and how we live must be closed. We must cultivate the peace of Christ as part of strengthening the connections between faith and everyday life.

We close the gap between our claims of peace and our actual experience of it by maintaining our focus on Christ. Much as we place Christ at the center of our lives in order to experience balance, so we increase our inner peace by keeping our mind stayed on Jesus. We remember his example, his words, his life and ministry. Most importantly, we remember the gift of his sacrifice on our behalf and the gift of new, abundant, and eternal life that sacrifice affords us. As Paul said, "Since we have been made right in God's sight by faith, we have peace with God because of what Jesus Christ our Lord has done for us. (Romans 5:1, New Living Translation)

We close the gap between our claims of peace and our actual experience of it by doing God's will as well. Jesus said, "If you love me, obey my commandments. And I will ask the Father, and he will give you another Counselor, who will never leave you. He is the Holy Spirit, who leads into all truth." (John 14:15-17, New Living Translation) If God desires us to take a particular action in a relationship or other area of our lives, and we refuse to cooperate, we cannot know peace. If we pray for direction and receive that direction, but then do not follow that direction, then we cannot know peace. Faithful obedience is crucial to the nurture of peace. Again this reinforces the importance of strengthening the connections between our faith and daily lives. God desires us to live out our faith in the real world, not retreat from it, or practice our faith in a vacuum. Therefore, God must have room to move in our lives, to act and direct us in ways that only God can know. No matter how successful we become at our task of knowing God, we will never know God well enough to predict how God will act or what God is going to demand of us. Obedience is our necessary response. Through our obedient response and our determination to keep our mind stayed on Jesus, we will foster Christ's peace in our lives, and others will be able to see by our life posture that for us, God is the main thing.

Reflecting and Recording

Who is the most peace-filled person you know? What do you believe is the source of this person's peace? Make notes.

Using this person as a benchmark, what do you feel is missing from your life, or perhaps is robbing you of peace? Write enough to get this clearly in your mind.

If peace is dependent on keeping our hearts and minds stayed on Jesus, reflect on whether you are exercising the disciplines necessary to keep your relationship with Christ alive and vibrant.

✳

Spend the balance of your time reflecting on whether you may be resisting some call, or perhaps failing to respond to what you know is God's will.

＊

During the Day

Philippians 4:19 says, "This same God who takes care of me will supply all your needs from his glorious riches, which have been given to us in Christ Jesus." (New Living Translation) Memorize this passage and repeat it during the day as a way of claiming its promise.

DAY SEVEN: THE DIVINE DISCONNECT

Jesus replied, "The Kingdom of God isn't ushered in with visible signs. You
won't be able to say, 'Here it is!' or 'It's over there!'
For the Kingdom of God is among you."
(Luke 17:20-21, New Living Translation*)*

For the Kingdom of God is not just fancy talk; it is living by God's power.
(1 Corinthians 4:20, New Living Translation*)*

We have spent this week discussing the fact that our spiritual lives must bear fruit, that there must be visible signs that God is the main focus of our lives. We have focused on three areas in particular—justice, temperance, and peace—significant elements of the connection between our faith and our daily lives. Thankfully the power of sanctifying grace works within us to strengthen those connections and produce spiritual fruit in our lives. I close this week by highlighting what you may have already noticed—that somehow there is a "disconnect" between what God intends for our lives and our world and the reality of our lives and our world. It is this disconnect that may have even prompted you to begin this study in the first place.

I call this the "divine disconnect," and it was vividly illustrated for me in September 2002 in Oslo, Norway, when the World Methodist Council presented its annual Peace Award to Boris Trajkovski, President of the Republic of Macedonia. The award has been given since 1977 to persons who show courage, consistency, and creativity in working toward peace. Past recipients include

Mikhail Gorbachev of the former USSR, Nelson Mandela of the Republic of South Africa, The Grandmothers of Plaza de Mayo of Argentina, and Kofi Annan of Ghana. President Trajkovski received the award for his work in Macedonia, a country located in a region torn by ethnic, religious, and nationalistic divisions.

President Trajkovski is a committed Christian, and his commitment to Christ is evident in everything he does. This commitment was even noticed by a reporter from the German magazine *Die Zeit*, who wrote, "He is a Methodist lay speaker. He speaks like a Methodist lay speaker. Maybe that is why he dares to try to do the impossible." Listening to the president's acceptance speech, this divine disconnect became real for me as he spoke movingly about peace. It was clear that even though he struggles—sometimes successfully, sometimes not so successfully—to bring peace to his area of the world, there is a certainty within him of God's presence despite circumstances. It was clear that he is determined to keep his mind stayed on Jesus.

Time and again he emphasized that there is no true peace apart from the peace found in Jesus Christ. There will never be peace if we believe we are able to achieve that peace with our own hands. All we are able to do is manage conflict, not bring true peace. It is beyond us as human beings—sinful human beings—to achieve true peace because that can only be found in Jesus Christ.

In the midst of the struggles of his country and the pressure to lead his people, it was clear that Trajkovski's relationship with Jesus was a source of joy and peace. That was part of my experience of "disconnect"—talk of inner peace contrasts sharply with the outer violence and threat of war in our world today. The president's warning against talking too easily about peace emphasized the seriousness of that contrast.

There is obvious tension here. The peace of Christ is promised as a fruit of the Spirit; it comes from a certainty of God's presence despite circumstances as well as our determination to keep our minds stayed on Jesus. I have experienced it and seen it displayed in the lives of others. I know it to be true. Yet, there remains a huge disconnect between peace within and peace without. So how do we bridge the gap? How do we translate our personal sense of peace into something that affects the lives of others? There is no easy answer, but the question itself drives home the value of making God the main thing in our lives—of strengthening the connections between our faith and daily life.

We desperately need to bring our behavior into sync with God's will for our lives—not just to benefit our own spiritual life but because it is a crucial part of God's kingdom work in the world. Our dedication to making God the main thing in our own lives cannot simply be a private journey—it may be personal but it cannot be private. It must be translated into the world around us. Only then will we have a chance to do more than simply manage conflicts; we will have the opportunity to be channels of God's transforming power in our world.

Reflecting and Recording

Where do you see the largest "disconnect" between your faith and your daily life? Make notes in order to bring that area of your life firmly into your mind.

What steps might you take to bridge that gap? What might you do to bring your life more into harmony with your faith? How might others in your group support you in this endeavor?

During the Day

Take the first step in resolving the disconnect between your faith and your daily life.

GROUP MEETING FOR WEEK FOUR

Introduction

You are drawing to the close of this study experience with only two more planned group meetings. Your group may want to discuss the future. Would the group like to stay together for a longer period of time? Are there resources (books, tapes, periodicals) that the group might desire to use together? If you are a part of the same church, is there some way you might share the experience you have had with others? Test the group to see if they would like to discuss future possibilities.

Responsible participation is a requirement of being part of a group; however, the temptation often exists to "play it safe" and not risk being honest and vulnerable. Energy is another issue. Listening and speaking demand physical as well as emotional energy; so again, there is the temptation to hold back, to be only half-present, not to invest the attention and focus essential for full participation. I urge you to withstand these temptations. Your group sharing sessions are very important. Do not underestimate the value of each person's contribution.

In the King James Version of Philippians, Paul advises us to "let [our] conversation be as it becometh the gospel of Christ" (Philippians 1:27). Newer versions translate this verse, "Live in a manner worthy of the Good News about Christ." (New Living Translation) In the Elizabethan English of the King James Version, life and conversation are synonymous. That is an important word for us as we meet together. Life is found in communion with God and also in conversation with others.

Listening and responding to what we hear is very important. To really hear another person helps her to think clearly and gain perspective. It is life producing. When we speak in ways that make a difference, we speak for the sake of others, and thus contribute to the wholeness process.

Sharing Together

You are just past the midpoint of your workbook journey. As you anticipate your group meeting, spend a few minutes thinking about the experience in general terms. What is giving you difficulty? What is providing the most meaning?

- Reflect on your experience of "sanctification." Bring to mind significant events, changes, experiences, or relationships that have contributed to your sanctification.
- Think about your list of ways in which your faith is bearing fruit. What activities or actions make your faith visible to others? How might your faith life bear more fruit? What would you have to change to become more fruitful in your spiritual life?
- Think about ways we are robbed of peace.
- Ponder the experience of "disconnect" between faith and daily life. What might we do to resolve that disconnect?

Praying Together

While you may have viewed these weekly sessions as simply a time of sharing, they also are encounters with prayer. Jesus promised that whenever we gather in his name, he is present with us. We listen to others in love. We share, believing that we can be honest because we are loved and are gathered in the name and spirit of Jesus. So there is a sense in which, throughout your sharing, you have already been mutually praying. At the same time, there is power in a community verbalizing thoughts and feelings to God in the presence of those who share the journey. Let that be the case at your group meeting.

- In your group meeting consider calling each woman's name, pausing briefly after each name for some person in the group to offer a brief verbal prayer, focused on what that woman has shared. It can be as simple as "Lord, thank you for helping Julie to recognize the way you have been at work in her life," or "Loving God, give Carol the sense of your direction she needs to face the challenges she has shared." Don't forget to mention your leader.
- When all names have been called and all women prayed for, sit in silence for two minutes, opening yourselves to the strength that is ours in community. Enjoy being linked with women who are mutually concerned.

Week Five: Divine Destiny

DAY ONE: OUR KINGDOM NICHE

The truth is, anyone who believes in me will do the same works I have done, and even greater works, because I am going to be with the Father. You can ask for anything in my name, and I will do it, because the work of the Son brings glory to the Father. Yes, ask anything in my name, and I will do it!
(John 14:12-14, New Living Translation*)*

I believe that God has a plan for each of us. I am not talking about some sort of cosmic sense of predestination or fate. I am talking about a uniquely created purpose, an individual destiny, a divine destiny—divine because God created it for us. Our created purpose or destiny is the reason God designed each of us so carefully, with special gifts and talents. Discovering what that created purpose is should be a primary goal in our quest to make God the main thing in our lives. Without an understanding of our created purpose, without a sense of why God wired us the way God did and gave us the talents and gifts God did, we will continually struggle with the connections between our faith and daily lives. We will have no basis for understanding God's plan in connecting our faith with the activities that go on around us day after day. Jesus promised that we would do greater things even than he did. We will never be able to claim fully that promise for ourselves if we lack an understanding of what our purpose within God's kingdom actually is. We must discover our Kingdom niche.

Although the framework of this study does not allow me to focus fully on exploring our created purpose, I want to highlight a few important principles as we seek to find our Kingdom niche.

An important step in exploring our created purpose is to examine the gifts and talents with which God has blessed us. Not surprisingly, many women have difficulty with this basic component of self-awareness because they do not see themselves as "gifted." They have trouble pointing to any particular "gift." I believe this is because many of us miss one of the clearest signs of giftedness, *enjoyment.* The things we enjoy are frequently connected to the areas in which we have talent.

My experience with writing is an easy example of this. I love to write and am also fairly good at it. Yet, at one time I believed that to be able to use my writing in ministry would be "too good to be true." One of the tragedies of our current age is that we have lost a sense of the Holy Spirit working in our lives. I certainly missed it when I dismissed my enjoyment of writing rather than recognizing that enjoyment as the working of the Holy Spirit urging me to take something that I did well and use it for God's purpose. I probably would have been content to privately enjoy my writing if a colleague had not suggested that quite possibly God had blessed me with a love of writing precisely because God wanted me to use it as part of my ministry. What an eye opener that was! Using my writing as part of my ministry had seemed like a luxury, when actually it was a necessary part of the way God intended to use me.

God has blessed you with a unique assortment of talents. God has given you a love for something because God desires that you use that something as a part of God's overall Kingdom work. When we develop an understanding of how God has gifted us, we gain insight into our divine destiny—our Kingdom niche. We are able to see better what needs to be done in order to exercise those gifts as a deliberate part of our created purpose. For some of us that might mean moving into territory that makes us uncomfortable, or undertaking challenges that enable us to develop our abilities more fully. For all of us though, it never means taking on commitments that do not suit us.

I have a dear friend who wanted to sing in the choir at his church. He came to rehearsals and was warmly welcomed. After a few weeks, however, he realized that he just is not, and probably never will be, a singer. He decided that the choir was probably not a part of his overall Kingdom niche. Now he teaches a high school Sunday school class—something that he does very well and really enjoys.

Jesus promised that we would do even greater things than he did. By becoming aware of our gifts and talents, by opening ourselves to God's power to use those gifts and talents, we are able to grasp our divine destiny and find our Kingdom niche. Having done that, our faith and our daily lives will become intimately connected as God uses us for Kingdom work.

Reflecting and Recording

Spend some time assessing your gifts and talents. Make a list. Begin by focusing on the things you enjoy. Remember, joy may actually be the Holy Spirit working to guide you.

Reflect on your gifts and talents and the way your use of them might fit into God's created purpose for your life.

✳

Now look at your list. Focus on one of your abilities in particular. How might you use this gift for God?

During the Day

Act on your answer to the above question.

DAY TWO: LOCKED ON

*Jesus said to the people, "I am the light of the world. If you follow me, you won't be stumbling through the darkness, because you will have the light that leads to life."
The Pharisees replied, "You are making false claims about yourself!"
Jesus told them, "These claims are valid even though I make them about myself.
For I know where I came from and where I am going."*
(John 8:12-14, New Living Translation*)*

When pilots deploy missiles, they "lock on" to their targets. That means that the specialized equipment in the plane fixes the coordinates of the target to keep it in perfect range. Once the pilot has locked on to the target, he or she cannot miss; all that is needed is to push the button to launch the missile.

American archer Justin Huish won two gold medals in the 1996 Olympics. In the months following, he demonstrated his skill on one of the late-night television talk shows. To hit his target, he had to shoot through a garage, fire, and past two waving balloons that seemed to block his view. Justin pulled back his bow, closed one eye, and "locked on" to the target. He released his arrow and hit the bull's eye. Justin had locked on to his target; he was focused completely on it. What he was not focused on was the garage, the flames, and the waving balloons. For Justin, there was nothing between him and the target.

Jesus had that same kind of focus. He was locked on to his divine destiny. Even at twelve he understood his created purpose. When his parents discovered him missing on the trip home from Jerusalem they returned to look for him and found him in the Temple. "Why did you need to search?" he asked them. "You should have known that I would be in my Father's house." (Luke 2:49, New

Living Translation) For Jesus, there was nothing between him and God's will and mission for his life. They were always in his sight. He refused to allow the distractions of the world to block his view of God's created purpose for his life. He knew exactly where he came from and where he was going.

A student once asked Albert Einstein how many feet were in one mile. He shocked the class when he answered that he didn't know. The student was amazed that Einstein didn't know this simple fact and pressed him for why he didn't know. Einstein responded, "I make it a rule not to clutter my mind with simple information that I can find in a book in five minutes."

Albert Einstein wasn't interested in trivial data. His passion was exploring the deep things of the universe. He avoided the distractions of unnecessary information. Justin Huish was not interested in the garage or the flames or the waving balloons. He avoided distractions and kept his focus on his target. The problem for us is that we focus too much on the distractions. We would rather write a report about the size of the garage, the temperature of the flames, or what the odds are that someone could hit a target without completely being able to see it. The issues of the world become bobbing balloons that distract us from locking on to our created purpose and pursuing it as though nothing stood between it and us.

In 1983, the First Presbyterian Church of Concord, California, made a bold and daring move. It purchased the porno theater next door to the church. Naturally the community was thrilled, until it became apparent that the theater proprietors still had several months remaining on their lease. That meant that for almost a year First Presbyterian Church was the landlord collecting rent on an X-rated adult theater. That did not sit well with the community; but the church did not budge. It was locked on to its vision and was willing to be misunderstood and criticized in order to guarantee that the theater would be closed and their own vision implemented. Within two years, the old Galaxy Theatre was the Presbyterian Community Center. Where once degrading pornographic images flashed across the big screen, Bible studies and recovery groups now meet. (*PreachingToday.com,* submitted by Greg Asimakoupoulos)

God has a divine destiny created for each of us. It is up to us to explore our gifts and talents, our experiences and passions, in order to discover it. Once discovered, we must lock on to that destiny, living our lives in such a way that nothing stands between us and our created purpose.

Reflecting and Recording

What do you believe your created purpose is?

Are you locked on to that divine destiny or are there distractions blocking your sights? What are those distractions?

What do you need to do in order to lock on?

During the Day

Take whatever steps are necessary to lock yourself on to God's created purpose.

DAY THREE: WHAT'S HOLDING YOU BACK?

Once a religious leader asked Jesus this question:
"Good teacher, what should I do to get eternal life?"
"Why do you call me good?" Jesus asked him. "Only God is truly good. But as for
your question, you know the commandments: 'Do not commit adultery.
Do not murder. Do not steal. Do not testify falsely. Honor your father and mother.' "
The man replied, "I've obeyed all these commandments since I was a child."
"There is still one thing you lack," Jesus said. "Sell all you have and give the money
to the poor, and you will have treasure in heaven. Then come, follow me."
But when the man heard this, he became sad because he was very rich.
(Luke 18:18-23, New Living Translation*)*

What do you really want to do with your life? What is holding you back from doing it? Money—not enough? The money you have but can't let go of? Stubbornness? Fear? Are you worried about what people might think, of not measuring up, or even of failing? Is it your priorities? Are you spending too much time on things that may not be as important as you think they are?

I began this week by stating that I believe God has a plan for each of us. Jesus said that we were destined to do great things—even greater things than he did. (John 14:12) Unfortunately, our lives become cluttered with distractions so that we cannot always see God's plan for our lives. Or worse yet, we let the voices of the world convince us that we are not capable of accomplishing that plan. It may make us uncomfortable to admit it, but there are things in all of our lives that hold us back. As we discussed yesterday, distractions and other forces can come between us and our created purpose, making it difficult to "lock on." It is as though they have an invisible grip on us, hindering us and blocking us and holding us back from moving toward the future for which God has created us.

The things that hold us back can lay claim on us from the outside or from the inside. In the story of Jesus and the rich man that began our reading today we can see how someone might be blocked from God's future by outside forces. Jesus told the man that in order to gain eternal life he must sell everything he had, give the money to the poor, and follow Jesus. The man went away brokenhearted. When we hear this story, we automatically assume that it was the man's money that prevented him from grasping God's future for himself. Jesus' words about how difficult it is for rich people to enter the kingdom of God (Luke 18:24) emphasize that understanding. Yet I believe there is another message for us in that story—one that applies to all of us, whether or not we are rich. The rich man's problem was not necessarily one of money; it was a problem of *focus*. It was not his riches that held him back from God's future; rather it was his focus on those riches. He was locked on to his money instead of locking on to Jesus; and because he wouldn't change his focus, he was unable to see the incredible future God had created for him. As a result, he went away brokenhearted.

What is your focus? What are you looking at? It is an important question because wherever your focus is, whatever you are looking at, that is the thing that will either hold you back or move you forward. This is true because we are really only able to focus on one thing. In this age of "multi-tasking" we like to tell ourselves that we can focus on multiple things at the same time; but when all is said and done, we are not really *focused* on all those tasks at the same time. We choose one, and the others are moved to the periphery. We are aware of them, but not focused on them. Have you ever been to a sports-oriented restaurant where there are many different television sets? It is easy to watch them if they are all on the same channel; but if they are all on different channels, it is impossible to watch them all at the same time. Or, how about conversing with someone who is also trying to read or watch television or do some other task. They may be focused on you for a while, but inevitably their focus will shift because they cannot fully focus on you *and* the other task at the same time. The reality is that we must always choose the one thing that is going to receive our focus, our full attention.

What have you chosen to focus on? Money? Career? Family? House? Yard? Boat? Next vacation? What are your priorities? Are you spending too much time on things that may not be as important as you think they are? Our focus can set us free to pursue the future that God has created for us, or it can hold us back from that created purpose. Making God the main thing in our lives enables us to be focused on the life-giving possibilities God has laid out for us, to see the purpose for which we were created, to discover the reason we were wired a particular way and given certain talents and gifts. If our focus is not on God, we will be like the rich man who went away brokenhearted, never able to completely grasp the incredible future God has created for each of us.

Reflecting and Recording

Look at your calendar of activities and commitments for the next several weeks. What does it tell you about your focus? How do you feel about that focus? Is it moving you forward or holding you back? Be honest with yourself. These personal reflections are for your eyes only, unless you choose to share them with someone else.

Now make a list of the various commitments you have made recently. How has your faith entered into your decision-making? How will these commitments affect your faith walk? As you review your list, reflect on whether each commitment hinders or energizes your faith development. Decide how you might remove yourself from those commitments that are holding you back.

During the Day

Take whatever action is necessary to begin removing yourself from any commitments that are hindering your faith walk.

DAY FOUR: OUR OWN WORST ENEMY

Jesus watched him go and then said to his disciples, "How hard it is for rich people
to get into the Kingdom of God! It is easier for a camel to go through
the eye of a needle than for a rich person to enter the Kingdom of God!"
Those who heard this said, "Then who in the world can be saved?"
He replied, "What is impossible from a human perspective is possible with God."
(Luke 18:24-27, New Living Translation*)*

There are many things that can hold us back from pursuing the purpose for which God has created us, both on the inside and on the outside. Yesterday, we talked about outside forces. Today we turn to those things on the inside that prevent us from claiming our future. We absorb all kinds of messages from the world. "It will never work." "You can't do that." The world has all kinds of negative descriptions for us that we internalize—untrained, too old, too young, too shy. By internalizing these messages and descriptions we become our own worst enemy. We hold ourselves back from discovering our Kingdom niche.

There was a preacher who visited China with a tour group. They were traveling in a bus along a snowy, muddy road. Suddenly a bus in front of them skidded off the road and tipped over in a rice field. The preacher immediately got off of his bus, ran to the overturned bus, and jumped on top. There were shattered windows, people were hurt; but the emergency door was facing up, so he quickly grabbed the handle. The door would not open. He pulled with all his might, but it would not budge. Others came to help, so the preacher gave up on the door and started helping people out through the windows. Then he saw another man go to the emergency door, turn the handle, and easily open the door. The preacher suddenly realized why the door would not open for him —he had been standing on it as he was trying to open it. (*PreachingToday.com*, submitted by Charles Chu)

This preacher had great intentions of saving lives, but he was the biggest obstacle blocking the door to rescue. That is how it can be for us. We become the largest obstacle in grasping our divine destiny. We are the ones holding us back from discovering our Kingdom niche. What we think about ourselves becomes a dead weight that can hold us back from real life.

The Scripture passage that began our reading today occurs immediately after the rich man left Jesus. Jesus told the disciples that it is difficult for the rich to get into the kingdom of God because they are so focused on their money that they cannot see anything else. In Eugene Peterson's rendering of this passage in *THE MESSAGE*, he describes the rich man this way: "He was holding on tight to a lot of things and not about to let them go." Peterson has described many of us. We are holding tight to all kinds of messages and descriptions of ourselves, and we are not about to let them go. And because of those messages we absorb Jesus' word about the rich and apply it to ourselves—it would be easier for a camel to get through the eye of a needle than for God to love me because I eat too much. It would be easier for a camel to get through the eye of a needle than for God to love me because I smoke. Because I drink too much. Because I'm divorced. I never went to college. I don't know anything about the Bible. Because . . . because . . . because. Sadly, we forget the last thing Jesus says in this situation: "What is impossible from a human perspective is possible with God."

During Week Two we talked about God's grace. The fact that God loves us exactly the way we are, regardless of our circumstances, regardless of our past, regardless of whatever "because" you use to describe yourself. Last week, we revisited God's grace in our discussion of sanctification. God loves each of us and desires to transform us into the person God created us to be—to recreate us in order that we fulfill the unique purpose God created for our lives.

A sculptor was interviewed on PBS. She had become intrigued by the eye-of-the-needle story. She created a huge piece of sculpture by putting a thimble through the eye of a needle. She accomplished this feat by stretching the thimble out until it was eighteen feet long, then threading it through the needle. As she was describing this, the interviewer commented, "I guess that's what God does to the rich man." The artist laughed and said, "Yes, stretched him way out."

That is exactly what God does to us. God stretches and pulls and molds and shapes us until we can fit through the eye of a needle, until we are just the right shape to participate in the divine destiny created for each of us. God wants to reshape us, to open the emergency door that keeps us from moving toward our future. God is only waiting for us to get off the door!

Reflecting and Recording

Take a moment to think about what kind of messages and descriptions the world has given you that you have made your own.

$$*$$

Look back at the list of abilities you made on Day One. How does this list contrast with the messages you have received?

Close your time by writing a prayer asking God to erase those messages and descriptions from your heart and mind, to reshape you in order that you might better grasp God's future for you.

During the Day

On Day One you chose a particular gift and began working to use that gift for God. Continue those efforts. On Day Three you began the process of removing yourself from commitments that are hindering your faith development. Continue those efforts as well. As you work to bring your commitments into alignment with God's purpose for your life, remember that Jesus said, "What is impossible from a human perspective is possible with God." Cut this from the back of the workbook and place it where it will encourage you regularly.

DAY FIVE: THE POWER TO DO

*Jesus was at Bethany in the house of Simon the leper; he was at dinner when
a woman came in with an alabaster jar of very costly ointment, pure nard.
She broke the jar and poured the ointment on his head. Some who were there said
to one another indignantly, "Why this waste of ointment? Ointment like this could
have been sold for over three hundred denarii and the money given to the poor";
and they were angry with her. But Jesus said, "Leave her alone. Why are you
upsetting her? What she has done for me is one of the good works. You have the
poor with you always, and you can be kind to them whenever you wish,
but you will not always have me. She has done what was in her power to do:
she has anointed my body beforehand for its burial. I tell you solemnly,
wherever throughout all the world the Good News is proclaimed,
what she has done will be told also, in remembrance of her."
(Mark 14:3-9, THE JERUSALEM BIBLE)*

Integral to discovering God's created purpose for our lives is the issue of
power. If we are to gain a sense of God's plan, we must also gain a sense of our
power. We may not always feel it, but God has given each of us inner
power—the ability to achieve purpose. History has shown society's tendency to
try to take away our sense of power—sometimes by deception, sometimes by
sheer force. Yet, God has given us a gift of power, and recognizing it is crucial
to finding our Kingdom niche.

Discerning our inner power enables us to act boldly in the present as we seek
to make connections between our faith and our daily lives. As we exercise our
power in the present, we are also able to worry less about the future, knowing

that God is guiding that future. Helen Bruch Pearson describes the connection between our inner power and our daily lives in her reflections about the witness of Scripture. She writes, "The voices of my unnamed sisters from long ago in the Gospels have taught me to be less anxious about tomorrow when I have done what is in my power to do today." (Helen Bruch Pearson, *Do What You Have the Power to Do: Studies of Six New Testament Women,* Upper Room Books, 1992; page 12)

Do what you have the power to do today. The statement comes from the story about the woman who anointed Jesus with oil, the story that began our reading. This woman acted boldly in entering a gathering to which she had not been invited, in breaking the rigid social constraints and protocol that restricted women's behavior during that time in history, in asserting herself enough to touch and anoint Jesus without asking. She realized somehow that the time to do something for Jesus was quickly passing. If she was to act in any way, she had to act now. But what could she do? She was only a woman, with little or no power of her own. But as Jesus said, she did what was in her power to do; "she poured a senseless amount of precious perfumed ointment over Jesus' head." (Pearson, page 46)

Each of us has the power to do *something*—something that is uniquely ours to do. "We may not be able to do very much, or we may be able to do a great deal. The amount is irrelevant. God asks only that we do what we have the power to do." (Reisman, *The Christ-Centered Woman: Finding Balance in a World of Extremes*; page 94)

The good news is that our power is always magnified by God's power. Our inner power, which is in itself a gift from God, is augmented by God's own power. When I had been in ministry only a few years—still very much part-time as my children were young—I attended an evangelism conference. It was a powerful experience. I was surrounded by talented people who were doing exciting things for God. The last event of the conference included dynamic music and outstanding preaching; it was an awesome experience of worship ending in a time of group prayer with people spontaneously offering their prayers aloud. As more people prayed, I had the intense feeling of God's presence—not just in the service but also within me. I realized that what I was currently doing was not all that God had in store for me. As the praying continued the spiritual depth in the room overwhelmed me. I felt completely out of my league, and I was overcome by an intense feeling of unworthiness and inability. I felt utterly ill-equipped to do what God was calling me to do—reach out to non-Christians, nurture the spirits of newcomers to the faith. In that moment I was ready to abandon the entire thing; I wanted to get out of that room as quickly as I could. But then I felt the full weight of God's power on me; I couldn't move. I wanted to run, but I couldn't budge; I had to sit down. With people standing and praying all around me, I heard God's word to me, "None of that matters. You may be ill-equipped. I know you do not have all the ability. But none of that matters. You will do what you are able, and I will do the rest. I am your source of power and strength. It is not you who is working; it is me working through you." As time has passed, the power and truth of God's words have become clear. The focus of my current ministry, preaching at a weekly "seeker" worship service, affirms for me God's power to work through me. I am doing what I am able; God continues to be faithful in doing the rest.

We all have a life purpose, created by God especially for us. God has been crafting it for you since you were born, wiring you a particular way, giving you special gifts and talents. Making God the main thing in our lives enables us to receive the guidance we need, to do what we have the power to do; and it opens us to receiving God's power to sustain and strengthen us. In this way we are able to make the connections between our faith and our daily lives, *act* on those connections, and find the niche in the Kingdom that only we can fill.

Reflecting and Recording

The Christ-Centered Woman says: "The scope of our abilities is always magnified by God's power. There is always room for God to use us to do great and tremendous things—things that we never thought we could do. Those great things, however, are often composed of many smaller things, things that *are* in our power to do." (page 89) How do you see your current activities fitting into the larger work of God? What "small" things are you doing that are a part of God's larger plan?

If you applied the concept, "Do what you have the power to do today," to your life, what things might you begin doing?

How might that concept give you more confidence and boldness?

During the Day

Do what you have the power to do today.

DAY SIX: BIGGER THAN YOU

"The Israelite cry for help has come to me, and I've seen for myself how cruelly they're being treated by the Egyptians. It's time for you to go back: I'm sending you to Pharaoh to bring my people, the People of Israel, out of Egypt."
Moses answered God, "But why me? What makes you think that I could ever go to Pharaoh and lead the children of Israel out of Egypt?"
"I'll be with you," God said. "And this will be the proof that I am the one who sent you: When you have brought my people out of Egypt, you will worship God right here at this very mountain."
(Exodus 3:9-12, THE MESSAGE)

We have spent this week exploring the truth that God has created a purpose for each of us that can be discovered when we examine our gifts and talents, our passions and joys. Many things can hinder us from grasping God's future, our external focus, internalized negative messages and thoughts, the lack of a sense of power. Today, I want to focus on our life picture. Each of us has a picture of the way our life is or might become. The problem is that our life pictures are always limited. We ground them on what we believe we can accomplish with our own strength and resources. In our Scripture for today, Moses had a life picture, but it did not involve leading God's efforts to liberate Israel from slavery—"Who am I to appear before Pharaoh?" (Exodus 3:11, New Living Translation) Yesterday, I told the story of my experience at the evangelism conference. At that time my life picture involved only ministry to which I was already accustomed, but it did not involve the many other things that God had in mind for me.

As Christians we serve a mighty God, the creator of the universe, a God who is bigger than we can possibly imagine. It is that mighty God who has created our divine destiny, a destiny that is also bigger than we can imagine. Where our life pictures are *rooted* in common sense, the mighty God we serve has created a purpose for our lives that almost always *defies* common sense. Do you recall the story of Jesus' friend Lazarus who died before Jesus got there? When Jesus arrived, he told the people to open the tomb; but Lazarus's sister, Martha, who like us, was limited by common sense says, "Lord, by now the smell will be terrible because he has been dead for four days." (John 11:39, New Living Translation) Common sense holds us back from moving beyond our own life picture, toward the picture that God has for our future. Martha could not move beyond her common sense, which told her what a four-day-old dead body would be like. Jesus had to remind her of God's picture. "Didn't I tell you that you will see God's glory if you believe?" he asked her. (Verse 40)

The common sense that informs our life picture tells us, "I'm too old," "I don't have a degree," "It doesn't make sense." But our created purpose does not stem from what we can imagine about ourselves. It stems from what God imagines about us—and that is always bigger, always better.

As Moses continues to argue with God about sending him on this mission, he protests, "O LORD, I'm just not a good speaker. I never have been, and I'm not now. . . . I'm clumsy with words." (Exodus 4:10, New Living Translation) We tend to echo that when we finally catch a glimpse of God's purpose for our lives, "God, I could never do that; I'm not bright enough. . . . I've been divorced. . . . I'm in recovery." But again, God's response makes it clear that our picture is just too small, too limited. It shows us that God not only will be with us as we pursue our future, God will provide us with exactly what we need, when we need it:

"Who makes mouths?" the LORD asked him. "Who makes people so they can speak or not speak, hear or not hear, see or not see? Is it not I, the LORD? Now go, and do as I have told you. I will help you speak well, and I will tell you what to say."
(Exodus 4:11-12, New Living Translation*)*

God, the creator of our future, provides us with the tools we need to undertake that future—not only in furnishing us with gifts and talents but in giving us ordinary tools in our everyday life experience, tools we may not recognize as significant. When Moses encountered God in the burning bush, he was carrying a shepherd's staff, an ordinary stick that shepherds use every day. God told Moses to throw it to the ground; and when he did, God turned it into a snake. That ordinary staff became the source of extraordinary signs and wonders when Moses finally confronted Pharaoh.

We move from our limited life picture toward God's created purpose when we recognize that God takes the ordinary and makes it extraordinary. I grew up in the church and was often bored on Sunday mornings. I do not believe that was an accidental experience. Throughout my life I've had and continue to have many unchurched friends. I don't believe that is an accident either. My passion in ministry is to reach out to unchurched folks, to create worship experiences that are relevant rather than boring. That is how God works. God takes the ordinary and makes it extraordinary. Michael Slaughter uses an equation to illustrate it: Our ordinary experience and passion, plus God's presence, equals a mighty work.

God's purpose for our lives is always bigger and better than we can imagine when we limit ourselves to common sense, when we remain bound by the seeming ordinariness of our experience. Yet, God uses that ordinariness for his purposes when we open ourselves to God's picture for our lives, reminding ourselves that it is not how we imagine ourselves that is so crucial to grasping our future; it is how God imagines us that counts.

Reflecting and Recording

Reflect for a few minutes on your life experience—the ordinary elements of your current daily activities as well as your past. Make a list of some of these as they come to your mind.

✳

Now reflect on your passions. What is it about life that excites you or ener-gizes you? Make a list of these passions.

*

Look at your two lists. How might God use these ordinary experiences and passions for God's purpose? How might you use those ordinary experiences and passions in your quest to make stronger connections between your faith and your daily life?

During the Day

Slaughter's equation is printed in the back of the workbook. Cut it out and put it somewhere prominate to remind you that it is not how you imagine your-self; it is how God imagines you.

DAY SEVEN: WHEN DID ALL THESE BASEBALL PLAYERS GET HERE?

The time is fulfilled, and the kingdom of God is at hand.
Repent, and believe the gospel.
(Mark 1:15, New King James Version*)*

Earlier this week we explored the concept of locking on to our created purpose. As we conclude this week, I want to explore how locking on to that purpose enables us to see how we fit into God's overall kingdom work. One of my favorite movies is *Field of Dreams* with Kevin Costner and James Earl Jones. Costner's character, Ray Kinsella, is "inspired by a voice he can't ignore to pursue a dream he can hardly believe." (Video Jacket promotion, *Field of Dreams,* A Gordon Company Production, MCA/Universal Home Video, 1989) Despite the fact that everyone thinks he is crazy and his banker brother-in-law is threatening to foreclose on his farm, Ray builds a baseball diamond in the middle of his cornfield in Iowa. He can see something breaking into the ordinary reality of life; he does not know exactly what it is, but he trusts his inner feelings and moves forward anyway. He is locked on to his dream. As the movie unfolds, we discover the reality that there is something incredibly special about Ray's baseball field in the middle of Iowa—it draws baseball legends from long ago to play, a reality that can be seen and experienced by people who trust and believe in the larger vision. We also discover that the distractions of the world prevent other people from seeing the larger vision; and because they allow themselves to be distracted, they miss out on an amazing experience.

The good news of Jesus Christ is that the kingdom of God is here among us. The mystery is that while the kingdom of God is here, it is also not yet here. The good news is that the kingdom of God is visible. The mystery is that while the kingdom of God is visible, we see it as though we are looking through a dim mirror. Ray does not know why he is building a baseball field; he just knows he has to do it. Then a reason starts to become clear: People will come; they will pay to come. Terence Mann (played by James Earl Jones) says in an inspiring soliloquy that they will not mind paying because "it's money they have but peace they lack."

In a climactic scene, as Ray's brother-in-law, who has up until now been unable to see any of the activity taking place on the field, is arguing with him about giving it all up, trying to convince him to sign papers to sell the farm and avoid foreclosure. Ray realizes he has to go through with it. He is locked on to his dream and is willing to risk foreclosure in order to see it through. As they argue, Ray's young daughter loses her balance and falls from the top seat of the bleachers. The ensuing crisis and resulting interaction with the baseball players changes the entire dynamic. When it is clear that the young girl will be fine, Ray's brother-in-law suddenly looks around and asks, "When did all these baseball players get here?"

God desires that God's kingdom come soon. God yearns for the "not yet" of God's kingdom to become fully realized and wants us to be part of the plan to make it happen. When we begin making strong connections between our faith and our daily life, when we recognize our created purpose and enter into partnership with God in moving toward that purpose, we enter into God's kingdom work. When we become an active part of that plan, God's kingdom unexpectedly bursts into our consciences—when did all these baseball players get here? Suddenly we can see that God's kingdom *is* here, it is among us, we *are* a part of it, experiencing it and making it happen in partnership with God.

Reflecting and Recording

Reflect on the ways you have experienced God's kingdom breaking into our world.

✻

Now turn to the ways God's kingdom remains hidden, or "not yet." In what ways are you struggling to see the reality of God's kingdom? What is distracting you from seeing?

How do you feel your own life fits in as an active part of God's overall Kingdom work?

During the Day

Be alert to the ways God is working around you and through you to make God's kingdom come on earth.

GROUP MEETING FOR WEEK FIVE

Introduction

Last week you may have discussed possibilities for your group continuing to meet. To further that discussion, I would suggest two possibilities. The first is to select two or three weeks of the study that were especially difficult or especially meaningful. Go through those weeks as an extension of your time together.

A second option would be to decide to continue your group using another resource. It may be helpful to appoint two or three women to bring a resource suggestion to the group next week.

If this workbook style is meaningful, here are several other options as well:

- *The Workbook of Living Prayer,* Maxie Dunnam
- *The Workbook on the Christian Walk,* Maxie Dunnam
- *The Workbook on the Seven Deadly Sins,* Maxie Dunnam and Kimberly Dunnam Reisman
- *The Workbook on Virtues and the Fruit of the Spirit,* Maxie Dunnam and Kimberly Dunnam Reisman
- *The Workbook on the Ten Commandments,* Maxie Dunnam and Kimberly Dunnam Reisman

If your group would prefer a traditional book format, two additional resources might prove meaningful:

- *The Christ-Centered Woman: Finding Balance in a World of Extremes,* Kimberly Dunnam Reisman
- *Do What You Have the Power to Do: Studies of Six New Testament Women,* Helen Bruch Pearson

Another possibility is for one or two women to decide they will recruit and lead a separate group through this workbook. Many women are looking for a small-group experience, and this is a way to respond to their need.

Sharing Together

In anticipation of your meeting,
- Think about the concept that the joy we find in certain abilities may actually be the Holy Spirit urging us to take something that we do well and using it for God's purpose.
- Look back at the particular gift you listed as something you might use for God (Reflecting and Recording, Day One, page 129). How might the group support you?
- Reflect on what you believe to be your divine destiny. What are the distractions that are keeping you from seeing God's purpose?
- Think about what things you might begin doing if you were to apply the concept, "Do what you have the power to do today," to your life.

Praying Together

- As you enter a "season or prayer" at the close of your time together, consider reading the prayer you wrote during the Reflecting and Recording period of Day Four—a prayer expressing desire for God to erase negative messages and descriptions from your heart and mind and to reshape you in order that you might better grasp God's future.
- Move into a time of open prayer and feel free to offer a few sentences of prayer about any concern. This may take on the structure of "conversational prayer" with one woman's prayer stimulating another to center her prayers. That means you do not have to do all your praying at once. You may pray a sentence or two now about something that is on your heart. Later, someone else's prayers, or the direct leading of the Spirit, may stimulate you to verbalize other concerns.
- Spend as much time as necessary in this "season of prayer" with different women praying as they will. You might then want to close by singing a chorus or a verse of a familiar hymn.

Week Six:
The Big Picture

DAY ONE: STORIES RATHER THAN MODELS

All Jesus did that day was tell stories—a long storytelling afternoon.
His storytelling fulfilled the prophecy:
"I will open my mouth and tell stories;
I will bring out into the open
things hidden since the world's first day."
(Matthew 13:34-35, THE MESSAGE)

I closed last week by discussing the ways in which we become aware of our place in God's overall kingdom work. That leads us directly into the focus of our last week together—the idea that we have a part to play in God's overarching plan, a Kingdom niche in God's kingdom plan. In other words, our story uniquely fits into God's story. You may wonder how that concept connects with the goals of this study: to know God, to make God the main thing in our lives, and to strengthen the connections between faith and daily life. I believe they are connected because our success in reaching those goals depends to a large degree on the depth of our understanding of how our individual stories fit into God's divine story.

We began our journey in Week One by exploring Scripture because that is one of God's main avenues of self-communication. It is a natural place for us to close as well. Scripture undergirds all of our efforts to make God the main thing in our lives. It grounds our faith, our prayer life, our moral lives, the discernment of our life's purpose. Yet we must be cautious that we do not become so focused on the lessons that we lose the story—missing the forest for the trees, so to speak. Scripture was not meant to force a godly shape on our lives but rather to be a vehicle of God's transforming power. Eugene Peterson warns us about this misuse of Scripture:

Somewhere along the way, most of us pick up bad habits of extracting from the Bible what we pretentiously call "spiritual principles," or "moral guidelines," or "theological truths," and then corseting ourselves in them in order to force a godly shape on our lives. That's a mighty uncomfortable way to go about improving our condition. And it's not the gospel way. Story *is the gospel way. Story isn't imposed on our lives; it invites us into its life. As we enter and imaginatively participate, we find ourselves in a more spacious, freer, and more coherent world. We didn't know all this was going on! We had never noticed all this significance! If true— and the Bible is nothing if not true—story brings us into more reality, not less, expands horizons, sharpens both sight and insight. Story is the primary means we have for learning what the world is, and what it means to be a human being in it.*
(Eugene Peterson, Leap Over a Wall: Earthy Spirituality
for Everyday Christians, *HarperCollinsPublishers, 1997; page 4)*

Recognizing that Scripture is one giant, divine story compiled of many smaller stories opens us to the reality that our story fits in as well. Our story fits because life itself is a story. As Peterson asserts

Life itself has a narrative shape—a beginning and end, plot and characters, conflict and resolution. Life isn't an accumulation of abstractions such as love and truth, sin and salvation, atonement and holiness; life is the realization of details that all connect organically, personally, specifically: names and fingerprints, street numbers and local weather, lamb for supper and a flat tire in the rain. God reveals himself to us not in a metaphysical formulation or a cosmic fireworks display but in the kind of stories that we use to tell our children who they are and how to grow up as human beings, tell our friends who we are and what it's like to be human. Story is the most adequate way we have of accounting for our lives, noticing the obscure details that turn out to be pivotal, appreciating the subtle accents of color and form and scent that give texture to our actions and feeling, giving coherence to our meetings and relationships in work and family, finding our precise place in the neighborhood and in history.
(Peterson, pages 3–4)

Understanding the narrative nature of Scripture opens us to relating to God in *authentic* ways rather than in antiseptic theological terms best reserved for the academy. In exploring God's story and all the smaller stories within it, we learn not only *how* God fits into our real world, but the more foundational truth that God is actually *part* of our real world—we realize that God has immersed God's self in history. Instead of standing outside the story and hurling thunderbolts into it, God enters the story itself and invites each of us to freely participate in God's ways. Rather than giving us models, the Bible gives us stories—stories that tell us that to live life well we must deal with

danger and parents and enemies and friends and lovers and children and wives and pride and humiliation and rejection and siblings and sickness and death and sexuality and justice and fear and peace—to say nothing of diapers and faxes and breakfast and traffic jams and clogged drainpipes and bounced checks. But always, at the forefront and in the background of circumstances, events, and people, it's God. It's always God with whom we have to do. (Peterson, pages 4–5)

We are more alive when we are dealing with God than at any other time. As we delve into the stories of Scripture, as we deal with God and God becomes more fully known, we begin to see that God desires to tell a story through our lives—that our own story fits into God's grand story. As we discussed last week, we have a Kingdom niche in God's overall kingdom plan. We may not understand exactly how our story fits, but we are reminded that all the details, regardless of how disagreeable or seemingly inconsequential they may seem to us, are filled with meaning for the story.

Reflecting and Recording

Spend some time reflecting on several of your favorite Bible stories. Pull out a Bible and reread them with an eye for the "story."

✳

Make notes about why these stories appeal to you. What is it about them that you find compelling?

What insights about God do you gain from these stories?

What insights do you gain about human beings?

During the Day

Be aware of the details of your life as they unfold today; be open to understanding them as fitting into God's larger story.

DAY TWO: COMPETING STORIES, PART ONE

Furthermore, because of Christ, we have received an inheritance from God, for he chose us from the beginning, and all things happen just as he decided long ago.
(Ephesians 1:11, New Living Translation*)*

Attempting to see God's grand story as the context for our own smaller stories was at one time an easy thing to do; society for the most part viewed God as the all-knowing dramatist of the cosmos, writing the story of our lives and history. It was God's story that framed our own. Unfortunately, in this postmodern, post-liberal time it appears that we have given up the idea that there might be any one overarching story to explain life; instead we have chosen to be distracted by all the little stories that compete for our attention. The culture in which we now find ourselves is one in which no one seems to know the plot of the epic drama of history unfolding around us. No one even seems interested in *wanting* to know of an epic drama, an overarching story, or a grand narrative. Rather, we flit about from one small story to another, casting about for meaning but not completely able to find it. Kurt Bruner described our situation well when he wrote, "There are plenty of little stories competing for our allegiance but no one big story that can capture our hearts or explain our lives. Sadly, once we rejected the true myth, we were left with mere fables." (Kurt Bruner, *The Divine Drama,* Tyndale House Publishers, Inc., 2001; page 161)

When we dedicate ourselves to making God the main thing in our lives, to connecting our faith more deeply to our everyday lives, we must confront the reality of these competing stories. Just as we must explore our stance toward

Scripture and its authority in our lives if we are to begin to connect it with integrity to our decisions and commitments, so we must search ourselves to see what story has captured our imagination. Is it the divine drama or a mere fable?

Last week I probed the concept of a divine destiny that exists for each of us, a created purpose for which God has crafted us, giving us unique talents, gifts, and passions. As each of us seeks to understand that divine purpose and live it fully and deliberately, we must make sure that we remain firmly rooted in God's overarching story. If, in pursuit of our future, we ground ourselves on fable rather than on truth, we risk disappointment and disillusionment if our desires and passions are not completely fulfilled.

The movie *Dead Poets Society* (United States: Buena Vista Pictures Distributions, 1989) is another favorite of mine, various scenes of which I have used in worship experiences to illustrate a variety of faith lessons. Within the overall story are many smaller messages such as, "Carpe diem!" or "Seize the day!" and "Follow your dreams," which are valuable when viewed within God's divine drama. But there is an underlying element of tragedy when those smaller messages are removed from God's divine drama and placed within the context of fable. In the film, Robin Williams plays an unorthodox English teacher, Mr. Keating, who is a new teacher at a prep school for boys, which, not surprisingly, emphasizes diligence and conformity over passion and individuality. Keating's love for poetry emanates from him in dynamic and exciting ways, and his students are quickly inspired to enter into the passion for life by exploring what it means for them to "Carpe diem! Seize the day! Make your lives extraordinary!"

On the first day of class, Keating takes his students to the school trophy case. Inside the case are aging photos of young boys from decades past, very much like the current students. As the students gaze at the pictures, Keating explains why it is so important to seize the day saying, "Because we are food for worms, lads. Because believe it or not, each and every one of us in this room is one day going to stop breathing, turn cold, and die." He goes on to say that the boys in the photos are a witness to the fleetingness of life. Each of them began with grand dreams, but each of them is now cold in the ground, "fertilizing daffodils." Thus Keating frames the fable that grounds the various positive messages and leads to disaster for one student in particular: Make the most of every moment of your life while you can because life is short. And when it's over, it's over.

As the movie progresses, one student in particular dedicates himself to Keating's "make your life extraordinary" message. As he has grown, Neil has taken on the huge burden of his stern father's expectations, but in response to Mr. Keating, decides to throw off that burden and seize the day. He auditions for the lead in the school play. Knowing that he is directly disobeying his father by receiving the part, Neil decides to go ahead with the production, counting on the fact that his father will be out of town for the performances. We realize through Neil's wonderful opening night performance that he was meant to be an actor and not the doctor his father desires. Unfortunately, that is not how Neil's father sees things, even though he too is present for his son's great opening night performance. After the play, he informs Neil that he will be transferring him to a military academy in order to thwart any further exploration of acting. Obviously Neil is crushed, the small spark of passion ignited in his life suddenly snuffed out by his autocratic father; and while his parents are sleeping, he uses his father's gun to take his own life.

My first inclination is to be angry with Neil's father. How dare he hinder what surely must have been God's plan for this young boy? But as I reflect on the film, I begin to wonder. Certainly Neil's father was strict and seemingly unyielding, but it is also clear that he loved his son. Couldn't he have been acting in what he believed was Neil's best interest? Maybe the real villain is not Neil's father but the larger fable that was grounding Neil's individual story—that fable provided by Mr. Keating on the first day of school: We are food for worms, lads. Life is short; make the most of it because when it's over, it's over.

Rather than grounding his individual story on God's grander, divine story, Neil pledged his allegiance to a fable that told him that his life would have meaning *only* if he was able to pursue his passions. Clearly he believed that a life where he was not allowed to "seize the day" was not worth living. As we dedicate ourselves to pursuing God's created purpose for our lives, we must recognize that this is a sad replacement for God's divine drama. Very few people in this world are able to live the life of their dreams. Few of us ever get *all* that we want out of this life. Yet that does not render our lives meaningless.

In my last year of seminary I believed God was leading me to minister in the area of theological ethics. I had—and continue to have—a passion for it. Believing that God wanted me to use that passion, I applied for doctoral study. I wasn't accepted. It was a huge blow, not only to my self-esteem but also to my sense of God's purpose for my life and my confidence that my story really would fit into God's story. Had I grounded my own story on mere fable, as Neil had, I might have had a more tragic response to the disappointment of rejection. But I understood, albeit tentatively at that point, that my life was part of God's divine drama. I knew despite my disappointment that I was created for a purpose that would give my life meaning regardless of whether my own desire to pursue doctoral work was fulfilled. I had grounded my life on the truth that there is something above and beyond my earthly existence—when it's over, it's *not* over. I was part of something much greater than my own little story.

The world is filled with partial, or incomplete, or inadequate, or incorrect stories seeking to compete with God's divine story. If one of these has captured our imagination, we are destined for discouragement, disappointment, or worse. God has created a destiny for each of us, a unique purpose for which God has crafted us, providing us the appropriate talents, gifts, and passions to accomplish that purpose; yet how that future will unfold is not always clear. While we are to use our gifts, talents, and passions in seeking God's purpose for our lives, the use of those gifts, talents, and passions is not an end in itself; it is the means through which we faithfully seek our created purpose. As we seek to understand our divine purpose, to live it fully and deliberately, we must make sure we remain firmly rooted in God's overarching story, thus gaining meaning not from the isolated fulfillment of our individual passions and desires but from the unique place we hold within God's unfolding drama.

Reflecting and Recording

What is the larger story on which you are grounding your individual story?

Does this story reflect God's divine drama? Why or why not?

How might the disappointments and disillusionments in your life be connected to a dependence on the wrong story?

During the Day

Live today knowing that even when our individual desires and passions are not completely fulfilled, our stories fit into God's divine drama, and meaning can come in knowing that when it's over, it's *not* over.

DAY THREE: COMPETING STORIES, PART TWO

But Moses protested, "If I go to the people of Israel and tell them,
'The God of your ancestors has sent me to you,' they won't believe me.
They will ask, 'Which god are you talking about? What is his name?'
Then what should I tell them?" God replied, "I AM THE One WHO ALWAYS IS.
Just tell them, 'I AM has sent me to you.' " God also said, "Tell them, 'The LORD,
the God of your ancestors—the God of Abraham, the God of Isaac,
and the God of Jacob—has sent me to you.' This will be my name forever;
it has always been my name, and it will be used throughout all generations."
(Exodus 3:13-15, New Living Translation)

Yesterday, we explored the unfortunate reality that our culture has given up the idea that there might be any one overarching story to explain life. We have instead opted to be distracted by a variety of little stories that compete for our attention. We seem to have forgotten the plot of the epic drama of history unfolding around us; and rather than attempting to discover it, we flit from one small story to another, casting about for meaning but not completely able to find it. Today we explore a second competing story in order to firmly root our efforts to connect our faith to our daily lives in God's divine drama and avoid relying on mere fable.

A few years ago, Joan Osborne's song, "One of Us," received a great deal of radio airplay. (Joan Osborne, *Relish,* New York: PolyGram Records, Inc., 1995) At that time I used this song in worship to highlight a fable that is particularly popular in our culture today—that each of us can define our own view of God. Rather than connecting ourselves to a grand story that frames all of life, personal preference has become the fable that distracts us. The song posits the question, "What if God were one of us?" That is in sharp contrast to questions of earlier eras, such as "Who is God?" or "Which religion is right?" In our post-modern, post-liberal age, Osborne frames the question of our culture: If God had a name, what would it be? If God had a face, what would it look like? Frank McCourt, author of the popular memoirs, *Angela's Ashes* and *'Tis*, responds to those questions, reflecting the current stance of society, "I don't confine myself to the faith of my fathers anymore. All the religions are spread before me, a great spiritual smorgasbord, and I'll help myself, thank you." (Frank McCourt, "When You Think of God What Do You See?" *Life*, December 1998, as quoted by Kurt Bruner; page 165)

The cultural message that threatens to deprive us of true meaning is one that tells us that knowing God and making God the main thing in our lives is simply a matter of picking and choosing beliefs from the wide variety of worldviews; we keep the ones that we like and reject the ones that don't appeal to us. The competing story becomes the small story we write for ourselves, whatever we can create by piecing together the outwardly arbitrary experiences in our lives.

Kurt Bruner aptly describes the problem with this cafeteria-style approach to faith:

The problem, of course, is that reality is painfully indifferent to what any of us decides to believe. The law of gravity is just as tough on the guy who thinks he can fly as it is on the rest of us. Either God is or he isn't. Either there is a big story that gives life meaning or there isn't. What we choose to believe is irrelevant to what is or isn't true. (Bruner, page 166)

While what we believe may be irrelevant to what is or is not true, it is critical to how we view our place in the scheme of things. Bruner continues, "If the Christian narrative is life's true story—the transcendent myth all others seek to tell—then we are the supreme objects of God's affection. If it's not, we're something else." (Bruner, page 166)

At the beginning of our time together we asserted that we must explore our stance toward Scripture and its authority in our lives if we are to begin to connect it with integrity to our decisions and commitments. We need to understand our view of Scripture in order to avoid applying it haphazardly or only when it is convenient. In the same way, we must search ourselves to see whether we are experiencing God's drama as God has written it, or attempting to patch together an assortment of different scenes from other subplots in order to come up with our own script. Do we, in fact, believe the Christian narrative to be life's true story? Do we, in fact, view ourselves as the supreme object of God's affection? This self-examination is intimately involved with our discussion in Week Two, which focused on the basics of our faith—beginning your journey with whatever faith you have in that moment. We must ask ourselves whether or not we are traveling this journey with a faith in God's grand tale or somehow attempting to create our own script using other stories. This kind of examination is not as complicated as we might think, actually only involving a few very basic questions. First, does God exist? If you answer "yes," you are called a theist; those answering "no" are called atheists; and the "maybes" are agnostics.

The atheist's story will look a lot like Mr. Keating's "grab life by the tail because when it's over, it's over" fable. But the theist's story will read somewhat differently; a few more questions are needed to grasp it, however. If you are a theist and answered yes, God does exist, the next question is, "Is there only one God or many?" While polytheism (belief in more than one God) was widespread in ancient times, it is not as prevalent today. Believing in one God leads to a third question, "Is that one God a personal being who created everything?" Christianity, Judaism, and Islam assert that yes, God is a personal being who created everything; while Eastern pantheism and the variety of New Age approaches assert that God is not personal but rather an impersonal force of which we are a part.

As you might expect, answering in favor of a personal God leads to several additional questions that distinguish between the world religions. These include questions such as, "Does your God demand that you work to reach God or does your God pursue you?" Kurt Bruner highlights the distinction by asking, "Do we earn God's favor or does God win our hearts?" (page 168)

The answer to these final questions separates the Christian faith from all others. Recall our discussions of God's grace in Week Two. In the overarching story told by Christians, it is God who is chasing us, seeking to set us free. In all other worldviews, we are the ones chasing God, trying to redeem ourselves; but the truth is there will always be one more thing we could do to earn God's love and care—one more prayer that could be said, one more deed that could be performed, one more sin that could be confessed.

Knowing God and making God the main thing in our lives involves recognizing that there are many stories being told in our world. Each of them contains a different plot; each of them claims to be the true story. We deceive ourselves if we believe we can know God by piecing together these stories into our own smaller one. And we miss out on the profound truth that there is only one story with "the amazing scene in which the Author decides to lay aside his pen, enter the story, and play the hero." (Bruner, page 169) The gospel, God's overarching story of which we are a part, is the one story in which God redeems humanity rather than humanity struggling to redeem itself. Basing our journey on that story, rather than any mere fable that we can create on our own, will enable us to truly know God and discover our part in God's story.

Reflecting and Recording

In what ways are you attempting to pick and choose the elements of your faith cafeteria-style?

Walk through the questions for self-examination in the closing paragraphs of today's reading. Write your answers, including details about why.

Close your time in reflection. Reread your responses in the Reflecting and Recording sections of Days One and Three of Week Two, pages 47 and 53. Focus on God's efforts to win your heart rather than requiring you to earn God's love.

※

During the Day

Remind yourself once again of Maxie Dunnam's words, "When our minds are open to understand the Scripture, our hearts are open to receive God's grace. When our hearts are open to receive God's grace, our wills are softened to do God's bidding." Open yourself to the power of God's grace to make you a part of God's divine drama.

DAY FOUR: WHAT SORT OF TALE HAVE WE FALLEN INTO?

"I wonder what sort of a tale we've fallen into?"

"I wonder," said Frodo. "But I don't know. And that's the way of a real tale.
Take any one that you're fond of. You may know, or guess, what kind of a tale it is,
happy-ending or sad-ending, but the people in it don't know.
And you don't want them to."
(J.R.R. Tolkien, The Two Towers, *HarperCollinsPublishers, 1994; page 696)*

I deviate from my normal pattern of beginning each day with a passage from Scripture, because I believe J.R.R. Tolkien has an important word for us as we explore how our small story fits into God's grander tale. Growing up, I had always heard of Tolkien's *Lord of the Rings* trilogy but had never actually read it. However, in anticipation of the release of the movie version of the first book in the trilogy, *The Fellowship of the Rings*, I was determined to read all three before seeing any of the films. What an extraordinary adventure! Frodo and Sam, two tiny creatures—hobbits—set out on a dangerous mission to save Middle-Earth from the terror of an evil ruler. Being hobbits, they are a most unlikely choice of heroes, as hobbits tend to live out their lives quietly and contentedly, never straying far from the comfort and safety of their earthen homes in the Shire. Yet Frodo and Sam see themselves as participating in something far more significant than personal comfort and safety. They see their own stories, small as they may be, as part of a grander drama; and because of that view, they are able to push through their fear, risking everything as they confront unknown perils and threats, and continue their quest against overwhelming odds.

At one point in the second book, *The Two Towers*, Frodo and Sam, who have been separated from the rest of their group and are struggling to go it alone, sit down in a dark crevice between two great rocks. They wearily eat what they believe may be their last meal together before they go down into the Nameless Land. As they talk, Sam reflects on the fact that had they known what they were getting into, they might never have started their adventures at all—that "adventures" are not usually what we willingly pursue:

But I supposed it's often that way. The brave things in the old tales and songs, Mr. Frodo: adventures, as I used to call them. I used to think that they were things the wonderful folk of the stories went out and looked for, because they wanted them, because they were exciting and life was a bit dull, a kind of a sport, as you might say. But that's not the way of it with the tales that really mattered, or the ones that stay in the mind. Folk seem to have been just landed in them, usually—their paths were laid that way, as you put it. (Tolkien, page 696)

He goes on to muse that the characters in the best tales were probably like him and Frodo, faced with dangerous risks and given many opportunities to turn back. What made them great, he asserts, is the fact that they did not turn back. Because "if they had, we shouldn't know, because they'd have been forgotten. We hear about those as just went on." (Tolkien, page 696)

What a great word for us! As our lives progress, it appears that we simply "land" in the various plots that unfold, that our paths "were laid that way," as Frodo puts it. Having landed in these various plots, we are continually faced with choices—move forward or turn back. If we look at the most compelling stories, the ones that grab and keep our attention, there is often a hero who goes on to face danger rather than turning back to ensure a good end. Sam reflects, "We hear about those as just went on—and not all to a good end, mind you; at least not to what folk inside a story and not outside it call a good end." (Tolkien, page 696) There's the rub for us as our own stories unfold—the people living in the story would *prefer* to stay safe; but as Sam says, "Those aren't always the best tales to hear, though they may be the best tales to get landed in!"

The compelling nature of a good story is often the fact that while the people living in the story would prefer to stay safe, they are likely to face circumstances that require them to risk danger. The gripping element of the tale is that they do not know what lies ahead:

"I wonder what sort of a tale we've fallen into?"
"I wonder," said Frodo. "But I don't know. And that's the way of a real tale.
Take any one that you're fond of. You may know, or guess, what kind of a tale it is,
happy-ending or sad-ending, but the people in it don't know.
And you don't want them to." (Tolkien, page 696)

In the best stories, the main characters are like Sam and Frodo, woven into tales charged with uncertainty, where the stakes are high. The hobbits understand that they have an important role in what is unfolding, but they don't know how things are going to turn out. And as we read the story, we don't want them to know because that would take away all of the suspense and mystery.

Tolkien no doubt understood the potential inspiration Frodo and Sam would provide. Each of us is in the middle of a story charged with uncertainty; and if we're honest, we will recognize that the stakes are high. Like Sam and Frodo, each of us has an important role in what is unfolding. Unfortunately, also like Frodo and Sam, we aren't always sure what kind of tale we've fallen into; and we certainly don't know how it will end. The challenge is to recognize the possibility that seemingly obscure details may turn out to be pivotal; and more importantly, the parts we like least may, in reality, be the most significant elements of the story. On Day Six of Week Five I asserted that God's picture of our created purpose is always bigger than our own—that our created purpose does not stem from what we can imagine about ourselves but from what God imagines about us. Similarly, God may be writing a story for us that is bigger than our personal preferences, comforts, inclinations, or security. Knowing God more deeply enables us to understand that when the script of our lives doesn't turn out as we planned, it may be because it was not our script to write, but God's. And God is writing a larger story—an epic drama—and the details of our lives fit into that drama, even those elements that we would prefer to leave out or not experience at all.

Reflecting and Recording

Have you experienced a time in your life where you were faced with a critical choice—where choosing meant either taking the opportunity to turn back to safety or taking the risk of moving forward into the unknown? Describe that event. What was the outcome?

What parts of your story would you have preferred to leave out?

Looking back, have those parts proven to be crucial to your current story? How?

During the Day

Live today knowing that all of the details of your life, even the parts you feel are insignificant or unpleasant, are part of God's larger story.

DAY FIVE: ACTORS, NOT WRITERS

He thought of everything, provided for everything we could possibly need, letting us
in on the plans he took such delight in making. He set it all out before us
in Christ, a long-range plan in which everything would be brought together and
summed up in him, everything in deepest heaven, everything on planet earth.
It's in Christ that we find out who we are and what we are living for.
Long before we first heard of Christ and got our hopes up, he had his eye on us,
had designs on us for glorious living, part of the overall purpose he is working out
in everything and everyone.
(Ephesians 1:10-12, THE MESSAGE)

In our quest to connect our faith to our daily lives, we must recognize that we play a part in God's unfolding drama—a pivotal part. Yet, as we explored yesterday, God's drama is bigger than we are. Our own stories may be remarkable, but they remain subplots of God's epic story that is unfolding all around us. In the final book of Tolkien's trilogy, *The Return of the King*, Sam has a sense of this and wonders aloud to Frodo, "What a tale we have been in, Mr. Frodo, haven't we? I wish I could hear it told! . . . And I wonder how it will go on after our part." (Tolkien, page 929) When we recognize the grand scale of God's drama we realize that we are connected to something beyond the scope of our own small stories, something that will go on after our own part in the story has ended. That recognition empowers us to move beyond fainthearted efforts at self-preservation to bold acts of self-sacrifice and service.

Knowing God and making God the main thing in our lives involves recognizing that we are the actors in, not the writers of, our stories. As Kurt Bruner emphasizes, "My life is not the main plot of reality. When self-centered pride convinces me otherwise, my story becomes the timid and passionless pursuit of safety and comfort. The humble spirit, on the other hand, submits itself to a larger, transcendent story—turning life into a passionate adventure filled with purpose. Pride creates cowards. Humility inspires heroes." (Bruner, page 138)

This is important to our efforts to know God and make God the main thing. There may be elements of our lives that cause us pain, suffering, anger. We may not understand at any given moment how those particular aspects fit into the story God is telling. But our ability to accept that we are actors in the drama rather than writers of it, and to live out the part in which we find ourselves, is crucial to our life of faith.

Recognizing my story as a subplot is not meant to lessen its import. Our subplot is a pivotal part of God's epic drama. Frodo and Sam were given a part to play in the grand tale; it was not the entire story, but it was a part with a heroic purpose. If they turned back, the story would go on without them, but they would be forgotten. God's story will go on regardless of whether or not we are deliberate about living our own stories in the context of that great drama. Yet, we have been given an important part to play, a part that may not become clear to us until we leave the stage completely. How we play our part, our responses to the varying circumstances of our lives, will impact how our stories will be told. We can play our part with faint-hearted self-preservation or with heroic self-sacrifice and service. We can live out a timid and passionless pursuit of safety and comfort or a passionate adventure filled with purpose. Ultimately, God is the source of all of our stories. When we make God the main thing in our lives, we will be able to live not as the supposed writers of our own story—forever frustrated when the script does not unfold as we would prefer—but rather as confident actors within the drama of our lives, trusting that "long before we first heard of Christ and got our hopes up, he had his eye on us, had designs on us for glorious living, part of the over-all purpose he is working out in everything and everyone."

Reflecting and Recording

Have you experienced being connected to something beyond the scope of your own small story? Explain.

Recall Kurt Bruner's statement, "My life is not the main plot of reality. When self-centered pride convinces me otherwise, my story becomes the timid and passionless pursuit of safety and comfort. The humble spirit, on the other hand, submits itself to a larger, transcendent story—turning life into a passionate adventure filled with purpose. Pride creates cowards. Humility inspires heroes." Have you experienced this to be true? Describe your thoughts.

Frodo and Sam were given a part to play in a grand tale; it was not the entire story, but it was a part with a heroic purpose. How might recognizing your own story as being not the entire story but a part with a heroic purpose give you deepened meaning and boldness?

During the Day

In *THE MESSAGE*, Eugene Peterson translated Proverbs 3:5-6 this way:

> *Trust God from the bottom of your heart;*
> *don't try to figure out everything on your own.*
> *Listen for God's voice in everything you do, everywhere you go;*
> *he's the one who will keep you on track.*

Live today knowing that you are part of the overall purpose God is working out in everything and everyone. Clip Peterson's translation of Proverbs from the back of this workbook as a reminder that God is the author of our stories and will keep us on track as we seek to faithfully and boldly live the events of those stories.

DAY SIX: FOR SUCH A TIME AS THIS

Mordecai sent back this reply to Esther: "Don't think for a moment that you will escape there in the palace when all other Jews are killed. If you keep quiet at a time like this, deliverance for the Jews will arise from some other place, but you and your relatives will die. What's more, who can say but that you have been elevated to the palace for just such a time as this?"
(Esther 4:13-14, New Living Translation)

Long ago in a kingdom far, far away, there was a ruler who decided to throw the most extravagant party ever seen. He invited military leaders and noblemen, princes and provincial officials, and the celebration lasted six months! At the end of the celebration, the king threw a special banquet for all his palace servants and officials. This banquet lasted seven days and coincided with a separate banquet just for the women, hosted by his wife, the queen. On the last day of this week of feasting, the king, who was quite drunk, decided that everyone who was there should have the benefit of admiring the queen's stunning beauty, so he summoned her to come to him. Unfortunately for the queen, she refused to join him. As a result she was banished from his presence forever, thus prompting the search for a new, more worthy queen. Assembling all of the most beautiful virgins in the kingdom into a royal harem, the king's attendants began the selection process. Each girl received months of beauty treatments and then was brought before the king for evaluation.

Within the palace complex there also lived a Jew, Mordecai, who had compassion on his young, orphaned cousin, Esther, and adopted her as his own. Esther was exceedingly beautiful; so when the search for a new queen began, she was included in the royal harem. Before she left, Mordecai instructed her to keep her faith and family background a secret. The attendant in charge of the harem was very impressed with Esther and gave her special attention. As her beauty treatments and pampering progressed, Mordecai would visit her daily. When it eventually came time for her to go before the king, Esther's beauty shone through and "the king loved her more than any of the other young women. He was so delighted with her that he set the royal crown on her head and declared her queen." (Esther 2:17, New Living Translation) Even as queen, however, Esther followed Mordecai's advice and kept her faith and her family background to herself.

Time passed, and one day Mordecai was on duty in the palace and overheard a plot against the king. He passed this information on to Queen Esther who in turn informed the king, giving Mordecai the credit. The plot was foiled, and Mordecai received honor in the palace.

More time passed, and the king's prime minister, Haman, an arrogant and hateful man who was accustomed to having others bow to him because of his position, noticed that Mordecai, a Jew, refused to bow. This enraged Haman, who decided that it was not enough merely to punish Mordecai, he determined to wipe out all the Jews in the kingdom. He approached the king saying:

There is an odd set of people scattered through the provinces of your kingdom who don't fit in. Their customs and ways are different from those of everybody else. Worse, they disregard the king's laws. They're an affront; the king shouldn't put up with them. If it please the king, let orders be given that they be destroyed. I'll pay for it myself. I'll deposit 375 tons of silver in the royal bank to finance the operation.
(Esther 3:8-9, THE MESSAGE)

Thinking little of it, the king agreed; thus a decree was sent out that on a single day the following March, all Jews, young and old, including women and children, were to be killed.

When Mordecai heard of the decree, he sent word to Esther that she must act quickly on behalf of her people, the Jews. He urged her to go before the king and beg for mercy. This was a frightening prospect for Esther. She knew that the king would kill anyone who appeared in his inner court without being invited —even the queen—and the king had not called for her in over a month. What was she to do?

Mordecai responded to her concern with this fateful word:

Don't think for a moment that you will escape there in the palace when all other Jews are killed. If you keep quiet at a time like this, deliverance for the Jews will arise from some other place, but you and your relatives will die. What's more, who can say but that you have been elevated to the palace for just such a time as this?
(Esther 4:13-14, New Living Translation*)*

When Esther received his message, she made a fateful determination. Instructing Mordecai she said, "Go and get all the Jews living in Susa together. Fast for me. Don't eat or drink for three days, either day or night. I and my maids will fast with you. If you will do this, I'll go to the king, even though it's forbidden. If I die, I die." (Esther 4:16, *THE MESSAGE*)

After fasting, Esther went before the king, and was able to subvert Haman's plan to destroy the Jews. In the end, it was Haman who died; it was Mordecai who was honored; and rather than being exterminated, the Jews were empowered to defend themselves from any attack. All this was because a young girl's story unfolded in a way she could have never imagined, nor would have chosen; yet when it came time to play her part, she did so to perfection.

What are we to make of this story? There are many levels of meaning to be drawn from this story; but there is one nugget of truth in particular that is crucial for us as we strive to make connections between our faith and our daily lives. Mordecai did not call on Esther to intervene because she was the only hope for the Jews. Recall his words. "If you keep quiet at a time like this, deliverance for the Jews will arise from some other place." The Jews, God's chosen people, are an integral part of God's overarching drama. Mordecai knew this and knew that God would do whatever was necessary to avoid their complete annihilation. The vital piece for us is not what would happen in the grand tale; it is the decision Esther made as she played her part in that tale. Would she play the part God had chosen for her? Would she claim God's purpose in the unfolding of her own story?

Yesterday, I asserted that God's story goes on regardless of whether or not we are deliberate about living our own stories in the context of that great drama; even so, there will be times throughout our lives where we will find ourselves placed in situations "for such a time as this." Mordecai's call to Esther is also a call to us—not to save the day, but to fulfill a destiny.

176

Esther clearly saw her life as part of a bigger, grander drama and was able to face confidently the uncertainty of her future because of that knowledge. As our stories unfold, we may be faced with hardship and pain, joy and celebration, sorrow and heartbreak, pleasure and happiness. All of these aspects are significant and combine to enable us to grasp the future God has created for us. There may be times when we do not like our part in the story unfolding around us; but when we remain faithful, like Esther, we are able to do what needs to be done "at such a time as this."

Every aspect of our lives is part of God's greater drama—the mundane and even the painful. When we understand them in this way, they gain greater meaning; and we are encouraged to do the things necessary to deepen the connections between our faith and daily life, to come to know God more profoundly, and to fulfill God's purpose for our lives.

Reflecting and Recording

Esther endured much hardship in her life—she was orphaned, her people had been taken captive; even her role as queen was based primarily on the king's sexual desire rather than on any deep love, her life in the palace revolving around his sexual whims. Yet, the purpose of these hardships makes sense in light of her ultimate destiny. Reflect on your life. How might the events of your life, including the hardships, make sense when seen through the lens of God's divine drama? What purpose might God have for these elements of your story?

✳

During the Day

Be aware of circumstances in which you may have been placed "for such a time as this."

DAY SEVEN: THE CLIMAX

Shadrach, Meshach, and Abednego replied, "O Nebuchadnezzar, we do not need to defend ourselves before you. If we are thrown into the blazing furnace, the God whom we serve is able to save us. He will rescue us from your power, Your Majesty. But even if he doesn't, Your Majesty can be sure that we will never serve your gods or worship the gold statue you have set up."
(Daniel 3:16-18, New Living Translation)

You have spent the last six weeks exploring the variety of elements involved in knowing God and making God the main thing in your life. This week I have focused on the big picture—the idea that our own stories fit into the overarching story of God. I want to close our time together by reminding you of a very important truth. Every good story has a climax. That is the scene we look forward to throughout the entire telling or viewing. It is the part of the story where we finally understand how things are going to turn out—where we realize whether it will end well or badly—where we are moved to cheers or tears. The problem with our own unfolding stories is that the climax never seems to come. There never seems to be one point where we know how our story is going to end. To make matters worse for some of us, our stories seem to be unfolding more as depressing tragedies than happy-ending fairy tales.

One of my favorite Bible stories is about Shadrach, Meshach, and Abednego, whom God saved from the fiery furnace. Because these three young men and their friend, Daniel, were seen to be the best and the brightest Israel had to offer, when Babylon conquered Israel, they were forcibly taken from their family and friends and compelled to spend three years training for service to King

Nebuchadnezzar. Even though they had lost their freedom and had been taken into exile, they were determined to serve the king to the best of their ability because they trusted that God knew what God was doing. Because of their efforts, King Nebuchadnezzar quickly realized that they were better than any of his more experienced advisors and honored them appropriately.

Unfortunately, things began to turn sour when the king built a ninety-foot idol and demanded that all people in the kingdom worship it. Everyone was required to bow down before the idol; if they refused, they were to be put to death. As you might expect, Shadrach, Meshach, and Abednego refused to bow down and worship the idol and thus were denounced for disobedience. The story unfolds in the third chapter of Daniel when the three find themselves before King Nebuchadnezzar:

Is it true, Shadrach, Meshach, and Abednego, that you refuse to serve my gods or to worship the gold statue I have set up? I will give you one more chance. If you bow down and worship the statue I have made when you hear the sound of the musical instruments, all will be well. But if you refuse, you will be thrown immediately into the blazing furnace. What god will be able to rescue you from my power then? (Daniel 3:14-15, New Living Translation*)*

One of the reasons I love this story is because the king did not simply order Shadrach, Meshach, and Abednego to abandon their faith; he taunted God— "What god will be able to rescue you from my power then?" Such arrogant taunts always seem to have exciting results in Scripture.

Many of us have heard this story since childhood, so it is easy to zip through this section of the story in our desire to get to the climax. It is important, however, to think about what these three young men were experiencing at *this point* in the story—*we* may know what is going to happen next, but *they* don't. And the reality is that they were faced with the real prospect of being burned alive. Yet, despite that obvious terror, they courageously stood firm by responding with the words that began our reading today:

O Nebuchadnezzar, we do not need to defend ourselves before you. If we are thrown into the blazing furnace, the God whom we serve is able to save us. He will rescue us from your power. (Daniel 3:16-17, New Living Translation*)*

179

Once again, we are tempted to get ahead of ourselves because we know how the story turns out; but we lose an important truth if we rush on. Shadrach, Meshach, and Abednego did not describe what they *expected* to happen; they simply pronounced what was *possible*—the God whom we serve is *able* to save us. They were much like us in that they had little reason to expect a miracle. Many generations had passed since the days of miracles. The history they had experienced included exile and enslavement by an oppressive foreign power, and God had not intervened. Why should they expect God to act now? Of course miracles were always *possible;* but reality told them they were highly unlikely. That is why verse 18 is so significant, particularly as we are seeking to strengthen the connections between our faith and daily lives. In the face of this ominous penalty, being burned alive, these three young men boldly proclaimed, "But even if he doesn't, Your Majesty can be sure that we will never serve your gods or worship the gold statue you have set up."

We may believe that the next scene, the one in which God rewarded their faithfulness by rescuing them from the furnace, is the climax. But as we seek to make God the main thing in our lives, that is not where the significant truth is found. In God's divine drama the climax of Shadrach, Meshach, and Abednego's story is not the miracle. Miracles are not a big deal to God; rather they are part and parcel of being the creator of the universe. In God's eyes, the climax, the moment God has been anticipating throughout the entire story, is the moment Shadrach, Meshach, and Abednego proclaim, "Even if he doesn't . . . we will never serve your gods."

It may be difficult for us to see the climax of our faith story, but that may be because we are looking for it from our own perspective rather than from God's. If we look at the climax from God's perspective, it is most likely found not in God's miraculous rescue but in our obstinate determination not to lose faith. Kurt Bruner summed it up well when he said, "Our dramatic moment comes not when all is well but when all seems lost. The most profound dramatic question is not whether God will save the day but whether we will continue holding his hand if he doesn't." (Bruner, page 156)

From God's perspective the dramatic moment in Shadrach, Meshach, and Abednego's story was not when they walked out of the furnace completely unscathed; it was the moment they walked in—fully expecting to die. Likewise, the climax of my story will probably have nothing to do with the goals I achieve, how well my church does, how many books I write. The climax of our stories will probably be found in seemingly unnoticed choices we make in ordinary life —my husband's refusal to go along with a racist joke told by one of his patients because they are both white and the patient assumes John thinks exactly as he does, or my daughter's decision to befriend the new kid at school who has been continually left out, because she has heard stories of how Jesus reached out to all the ignored and hurting people he met.

Every time each of us exercises our will to live in sync with God, every time we choose to deliberately connect Scripture with the decisions we make in everyday life, all of heaven cheers. Those are our climaxes. Those are the scenes that God has been anticipating, those are the scenes God greets with cheers and tears. Making God the main thing in our lives is not about seeking out miracles or happy endings; it is about growing our faith so that it abides with strength even when to others hope appears to be gone. It is about living with joy and peace because we trust God even when God seems far away. It is about stubbornly refusing to let go of God's hand, come what may. When we commit ourselves to playing our part in God's drama, we are able to come to know God in a deep and abiding way and live with God as the main thing.

Reflecting and Recording

Spend a few moments reflecting on how you have been looking at your story —from your own perspective or from God's.

✳

How might viewing your story from God's perspective provide insight into the climaxes of your unfolding story? How might it give you boldness in your quest to make God the main thing in your life?

During the Day

Be mindful that a climax of your story just may occur in the living out of the ordinary events of this day.

GROUP MEETING FOR WEEK SIX

Introduction

This is the last meeting for your group using this study. You have already talked about the possibility of continuing to meet. Now is the time to finalize those plans. Whatever you choose to do, be deliberate about determining a timeline in order to facilitate a clear commitment from group members. Assign one or two persons to follow through with whatever decisions are made.

Your sharing during this session should reflect on the entire six-week experience. Begin with your workbook experience this past week, but save enough time to discuss your overall six-week experience.

Sharing Together

As you prepare for your group time, recall your favorite Bible stories and why you found them meaningful.
- How has that played a part in any disillusionment or disappointment?
- Reflect on the temptation to develop your faith cafeteria-style? Review your answers to the questions at the end of Day Three. (See Reflecting and Recording, page 165.)
- Think about the parts of your life you would rather have left out of your story and whether those parts turned out to be significant at a later time.

- Reflect on how the events of our lives, including the hardships, can make sense when seen through the lens of God's divine drama. Feel free to share about the purpose you feel God might have for particular elements of your story.
- Remember to take time to share what these six weeks have meant to you— new insights, challenges, things you need to work on in your life.

Praying Together

- As you conclude your group meeting with prayer, feel free to briefly express gratitude to God for something significant that has happened as a result of these six weeks.
- Consider sharing whatever decision or commitment you have made, or will make, in relation to knowing God and making God the main thing. It is important to be specific. As others verbalize their decisions and commitments, offer a brief prayer of thanksgiving and support.
- A benediction is a blessing or greeting shared between persons, or by a group, as a way of parting. The "passing of the peace" is such a benediction. Each person takes another's hand, looks into her eyes, and says, "The peace of the Lord be with you." As a response, the other replies, "And also with you." Standing in a circle, "pass the peace," and let it go around the circle.
- If you pass the peace as a benediction, afterwards consider speaking to one another in more spontaneous ways. Move about to different women in the group, saying whatever you feel is appropriate for your parting blessing to each one. Or you may simply embrace the person and say nothing. In your own unique way, "bless" each woman who has shared this journey with you.

Helpful Reminders

All Scripture is God-breathed and is useful for teaching, rebuking, correcting and training in righteousness, so that all God's people may be thoroughly equipped for every good work.
            (2 Timothy 16-17, Today's New International Version)

When our minds are open to understand the Scripture, our hearts are open to receive God's grace. When our hearts are open to receive God's grace, our wills are softened to do God's bidding.
                                                            (Maxie Dunnam)

When Christ is Lord of our lives, nothing else can be; when Christ is not Lord of our lives, anything and everything else will be.
                                    (Kimberly Dunnam and Maxie Dunnam)

What is impossible from a human perspective is possible with God.
(Luke 18:27, New Living Translation)

My ordinary experience and passion + God's presence = a mighty work. (Michael Slaughter)

Trust God from the bottom of your heart; don't try to figure out everything on your own. Listen for God's voice in everything you do, everywhere you go; he's the one who will keep you on track.
(Proverbs 3:5-6, *THE MESSAGE*)

Bibliography

Bruner, Kurt, *The Divine Drama: Discovering Your Part in God's Story,* Wheaton, IL: Tyndale House Publishers, Inc., 2001.

Dunnam, Maxie, and Reisman, Kimberly Dunnam, *The Workbook on Virtues and the Fruit of the Spirit,* Nashville: Upper Room Books, 1998.

Jones, Laurie Beth, *Jesus in Blue Jeans: A Practical Guide to Everyday Spirituality,* New York: Hyperion, 1997.

Manning, Brennan, *The Ragamuffin Gospel,* Sisters, Oregon: Multnomah Publishers, 1990.

Manning, Brennan, *Reflections for Ragamuffins: Daily Devotions from the Writings of Brennan Manning,* San Francisco: HarperCollinsPublishers, 1998.

Miller, David, *The Lord of Bellavista: The Dramatic Story of a Prison Transformed,* Great Britain: Triangle, 1998.

Pearson, Helen Bruch, *Do What You Have the Power to Do: Studies of Six New Testament Women,* Nashville: Upper Room Books, 1992.

Peterson, Eugene H., *Leap Over a Wall: Earthy Spirituality for Everyday Christians,* San Francisco: HarperCollinsPublishers, 1997.

Reisman, Kimberly Dunnam, *The Christ-Centered Woman: Finding Balance in a World of Extremes,* Nashville: Upper Room Books, 2000.

Tolkien, J.R.R., *The Lord of the Rings,* Great Britain: HarperCollinsPublishers, 1994.